"Brad Hambrick is a master of organization, strategy, and processes. *False Love* applies that mastery in a focused way to address sexual sin. In the past, I've steered people away from 'sin-focused' group counseling because of the common pitfalls that accompany many of them. *False Love* has changed my mind. With the wisdom and practical guidance of this excellent resource, groups helping people deal with sexual sin will not only avoid those pitfalls but can be a fount of encouragement and growth. Both as a counselor and as a sinner, I wish I'd had *False Love* years ago."

Curtis Solomon, Executive Director, The Biblical Counseling Coalition; program coordinator and assistant professor of biblical counseling, Boyce College; author of *Redeem Your Marriage* and *I Have PTSD*; cofounder, Solomon Soul Care and the Sentinel Institute

"Brad Hambrick has gifted us with a resource for tackling sexual addiction that is biblically sound and immensely practical. The journey out of addiction is often frustrating and lonely. *False Love* is like having a wise guide by your side every step of the way. I will be recommending and using this resource as a pastor and counselor."

Winston T. Smith, Pastor, St. Anne's Episcopal Church, Abington, PA; former senior faculty member, CCEF; author of *Marriage Matters* and coauthor of *Untangling Emotions*

"We found the *False Love* and *True Betrayal* group curriculum to be extremely beneficial for both the betrayed and the betrayer. Brad Hambrick's unique approach takes both spouses on an individual journey to self-awareness and healing. If you're wondering, *How did we get here?* and *What do we do next?*, this may be just what God has in mind for you. We can tell you, thirty-plus years post infidelity recovery, that healing is possible and worth every effort it takes."

Gary and Mona Shriver, Cofounders, Hope & Healing Ministries, Inc.; coauthors of *Unfaithful: Hope & Healing after Infidelity*

"With skill and precision, Brad Hambrick has given the church a much-needed road map to recovery and reconciliation from sexual sin and its disastrous effects. It's one thing to want to be reconciled after moral failure; it's another thing to know the way. *False Love* points the way forward and provides the confidence needed by all involved."

Joshua Waulk, Executive Director, Baylight Counseling

"I have been serving as a men's purity leader for nearly fourteen years, and I've witnessed many men experience freedom from sexual sin and develop a true relationship with Jesus. This book provides a comprehensive way to understand the depth and impact of sin, guides participants to the cross, and helps them walk with the Lord in purity, repentance, and freedom."

Ryan Silvey, G4 Men's Purity Leader

FALSE LOVE

9 STEPS TOWARD
SEXUAL INTEGRITY

Brad Hambrick

New
Growth
Press
newgrowthpress.com

New Growth Press, Greensboro, NC 27401
newgrowthpress.com

Cover Design: Faceout Books, faceoutstudio.com
Interior Typesetting and Ebook: Lisa Parnell, lparnellbookservices.com

ISBN: 978-1-64507-503-5 (paperback)
ISBN: 978-1-64507-504-2 (ebook)

Library of Congress Cataloging-in-Publication Data on file

Names: Hambrick, Brad, 1977– author
Title: False love : 9 step toward sexual integrity / Brad Hambrick.
Description: Greensboro, NC : New Growth Press, [2025] | Series: Church-based counseling
Identifiers: LCCN 2025012447 (print) | LCCN 2025012448 (ebook) | ISBN 9781645075035 paperback | ISBN 9781645075042 ebook
Subjects: LCSH: Sex—Religious aspects—Christianity | Integrity—Religious aspects—Christianity
Classification: LCC BT708 .H354 2025 (print) | LCC BT708 (ebook) | DDC 233/.5—dc23/eng/20250505
LC record available at https://lccn.loc.gov/2025012447
LC ebook record available at https://lccn.loc.gov/2025012448

Printed in the United States of America

29 28 27 26 25   1 2 3 4 5

Contents

What Is G4?

G4 is a peer support and recovery group ministry (e.g., like AA or Celebrate Recovery) built on two 9-step models that allow individuals to invest a season of their life in overcoming a life-dominating struggle of sin or suffering. G4 provides a safe environment where members learn insights and skills that will allow them to engage in biblical community more fully.

WHY THE NAME "G4"?

"**G**" is for gospel-centered groups. Rather than making an issue, struggle, or sin the centerpiece of our groups, we strive to make the gospel of Christ the core of all our groups. Our identity is not found in an issue but in an individual—the person of Christ.

"**4**" designates the four types of groups that will be featured:

1. **Recovery:** Groups for those struggling with a life-dominating sin, addiction, or traumatic life event
2. **Support:** Groups for those needing encouragement and support during a period of suffering or hardship
3. **Therapeutic Educational:** Groups for those needing information and resources about a specific life issue
4. **Process:** Groups for those needing help processing problematic emotions or multiple life stressors

SEVEN CORE VALUES OF A G4 GROUP

G4 seeks to uphold seven core values that help the ministry—both leaders and participants—care for and honor one another as they seek wholeness and holiness in their area of life struggle.

1. Bible-based and gospel-centered
2. Recognize the difference between sin and suffering
3. Built on honesty and transparency
4. Uphold confidentiality
5. Avoid struggle-based identity
6. Blend discipleship, accountability, and a guided process
7. Transitions into larger small group ministry

SUBJECT-SPECIFIC CURRICULUM AVAILABLE

G4 has ten subject-specific curricula available. Each uses one of the 9-step models, either sin or suffering, to walk through a process for finding wholeness and holiness for that life struggle.

Sin/Responsibility-Based Curriculum

1. False Love (sexual addiction and adultery)—bradhambrick .com/falselove
2. Gaining a Healthy Relationship with Food—bradhambrick .com/healthy
3. Overcoming Anger—bradhambrick.com/anger
4. Substance Abuse—bradhambrick.com/addiction
5. Anxiety/Depression* —bradhambrick.com/anxiety

Suffering-Based Curriculum

1. Anxiety/Depression—bradhambrick.com/depression
2. Navigating Destructive Relationships—bradhambrick.com /destructive
3. Taking the Journey of Grief with Hope—bradhambrick.com /grief
4. Trauma—bradhambrick.com/trauma
5. True Betrayal (processing a spouse's infidelity)—bradhambrick .com/truebetrayal

---

* Anxiety and depression are dealt with together so that each can be addressed from both a responsibility and suffering paradigm.

The 9 Steps of G4

G4 does not believe there is a one-size-fits-all solution to the struggles of life. Neither do we believe there is any magic in these sets of 9 steps. However, we do believe that these steps capture the major movements of the gospel in the life of an individual. We also believe that it is through the gospel that God transforms lives as he gives us a new heart.

In G4 groups, we attempt to walk through the gospel in slow motion with a concentrated focus upon particular life-dominating struggles. We do this in a setting of transparent community because we believe God changes people in relationships.

We believe that the gospel speaks to both **sin** (things we do wrong) and **suffering** (painful experiences for which we are not responsible) to bring forgiveness, comfort, and hope. We also believe that every person is both a sinner and a sufferer. However, we believe the gospel is best understood and applied when we consider how the gospel relates to the nature of our struggle. The 9 steps below are those used by G4 groups to address struggles of sin and suffering:

SIN-BASED GROUPS	SUFFERING-BASED GROUPS
STEP 1. ADMIT I have a struggle I cannot overcome without God.	STEP 1. PREPARE yourself physically, emotionally, and spiritually to face your suffering.
STEP 2. ACKNOWLEDGE the breadth and impact of my sin.	STEP 2. ACKNOWLEDGE the specific history and realness of my suffering.
STEP 3. UNDERSTAND the origin, motive, and history of my sin.	STEP 3. UNDERSTAND the impact of my suffering.

SIN-BASED GROUPS	SUFFERING-BASED GROUPS
STEP 4. REPENT TO GOD for how my sin replaced and misrepresented him.	STEP 4. LEARN MY SUFFERING STORY which I use to make sense of my experience.
STEP 5. CONFESS TO THOSE AFFECTED for harm done and seek to make amends.	STEP 5. MOURN the wrongness of what happened and receive God's comfort.
STEP 6. RESTRUCTURE MY LIFE to rely on God's grace and Word to transform my life.	STEP 6. LEARN MY GOSPEL STORY by which God gives meaning to my experience.
STEP 7. IMPLEMENT the new structure pervasively with humility and flexibility.	STEP 7. IDENTIFY GOALS that allow me to combat the impact of my suffering.
STEP 8. PERSEVERE in the new life and identity to which God has called me.	STEP 8. PERSEVERE in the new life and identity to which God has called me.
STEP 9. STEWARD all of my life for God's glory.	STEP 9. STEWARD all of my life for God's glory.

How to Use a G4 Series Book

Thank you for picking up a G4 resource. Books in the G4 series are a bit different from most books. Most books seek to *educate you on a subject*. By contrast, books in the G4 series seek to help you *navigate a journey through a life struggle*. With most books, if you understand the content, you are ready to move on to the next chapter. But in the G4 series, the goal is implementation more than education. You need to have "completed" a step, not just have "understood" its content.

For this reason, it is recommended that you work through this material with the help of others. The most common way that people work through this material is in G4 group, a lay-led counseling group hosted at a local church. You could also work through this material with a counselor or friend who is serving as a mentor. But because G4 materials take you through some of the hardest challenges in life, we strongly encourage you to enlist support as you traverse these pages.

G4 series books are the kind of literature you want to read with a pen, notebook, and Bible close at hand. This book will ask you many questions—the kind of questions that only you know the answer to, and the kind of questions that require reflection to answer. Take your time. The more honest you are, the more this book will benefit you.

This book also contains frequent devotionals that invite you to reflect on passages of Scripture. As you work through this book, we want to cultivate the habit of daily Bible study to find hope, direction, and meaning. Keep this book with your Bible and expect to move back and forth between the two as you read.

Often our hardships tempt us to rush, both mentally and emotionally. That means you may initially get anxious or frustrated as you work through this material. That's normal. Slowing down to reflect is difficult when life is messy. But it's worth it. Be honest about any impatience that emerges on this journey. Outside of the Bible, the best tool for change is simple honesty with people who care about you.

If you are not familiar with the 9 steps of G4, it is recommended that you review all the steps before you begin. Get the big picture of why this journey is laid out the way it is before you start working through the details of your struggle. You can find a 15-minute video overview of these 9 steps at the following websites:

- bradhambrick.com/g4sin for our sin/responsibility-based curriculum, used when a life struggle emerges from our choices, beliefs, and values.
- bradhambrick.com/g4suffering foroursuffering-based curriculum, used when a life struggle emerges from something we have little or no control over.

The *False Love* book is built around the 9 steps for sin/responsibility–based struggles. Too often we engage material like this through the lens of our fears and failures. As we read, we process each paragraph hearing our own self-doubt, the rejection of those we've failed, or the tone of those who have berated us for failing. This is especially true when life is hard. That is why we provide a free video teaching each part of each step at **bradhambrick.com/falselove**. Watching these videos before you begin each step will help you engage this material in the redemptive tone in which it was written. Allow these videos to offset the tendency to see things through the lens of fears and failures and to enhance your learning experience as you take this journey.

With G4 resources, we encourage you to use a consistent cycle to maximize your growth:

1. WATCH the video—use the QR code to find each video and hear the step in a redemptive tone.
2. READ the step—read the material to gain a clearer understanding of what you need to achieve in this step.
3. WORK the step—do the exercises and Bible studies to make and reinforce the desired progress.
4. DISCUSS the step—share what you're learning and how you're growing with a G4 group to learn from their experiences and how they navigated challenges like your own.

5. CELEBRATE progress—celebrate the progress you made and receive encouragement when progress is slow or you experience setbacks.

6. ADVANCE to the next step—move forward *after* you complete each step and surrender more of your life to God.

The graphic below is meant to provide a visual for this cycle. Most steps are broken into parts, so it is easier (not easy) to make consistent progress on your G4 journey. It is recommended that you use this cycle for each part of each step.

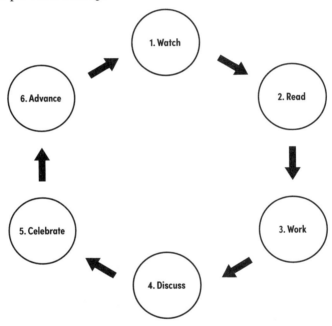

Figure 1. The Process of Working Through a G4 Curriculum

G4 series workbooks take the pace of Aesop's tortoise rather than the rabbit. Keep this in mind: Be content with progress and don't get impatient with your pace. Your goal is to finish the race. Consistent progress is the best way to ensure this happens and that the change you achieve is lasting. A journey this important is worth the time you invest to ensure you complete it well.

It's Not "Just Porn" or My Adultery
Partner Is Not "Just a Friend"

STEP 1
ADMIT I have a struggle I cannot overcome without God.

At the end of this step, I want to be able to say . . .

**"Not overcoming my lust and deceit would be more
costly than anything God would take me through
in the pursuit of his freedom. God is good for having
brought me to this point of admitting my sin."**

STEP 1

PART ONE

GAUGING MY MOTIVATION
AND COMMITMENT TO CHANGE

The video for this part of Step 1 can be
found at: bradhambrick.com/falselove1p1.

It is uncomfortable to talk about sexual sin. Even in recovery models like AA and NA, the sexual addiction groups still carry an additional stigma. But you've had the courage to start this journey. Thank you! That's not an easy step to take, and you're taking it.

However, considering the awkwardness around the subject of sexual sin, perhaps you hear yourself saying things like this:

- I can't believe we're actually going to talk about this. It makes me feel so awkward.
- I want to be rid of this sin and the shame it brings . . . but not yet.
- What would I do without this form of comfort when life gets hard and lonely?
- Maybe I should just manage my sin better . . . you know, just try to sin less until it eventually goes away.
- Why is it really that bad anyway? I'm not hurting anyone, and it helps me relieve stress.
- I'm sick and tired of feeling judged. God is the one who made me sexual. I didn't choose this temptation.
- I thought feeling loved and feeling good was a good thing. Why am I being condemned for it?
- When you show me a better way to guarantee I get what I need, then I'll listen.
- We're just friends. What's wrong with having friends?

> You've had the courage to start this journey. Thank you!

- I really care about them, and they make me happy. Doesn't God want me to be happy?
- I've prayed about this and think God wants this for me. I can see us having something special.
- Our sex life was getting dry, so I was just looking for a way to spice things up again.
- My life feels boring. I like to lose myself in the stories. It makes life interesting for a while.
- Do you mean to tell me that you don't notice attractive people?
- Men just need to be stimulated physically. It's part of our nature, not a choice I'm making.
- Women just need to be stimulated relationally. It's part of our nature, not a choice I'm making.
- I think I like the thrill of getting away with something as much as anything else. Risk is fun.
- If I get serious about changing, it could jeopardize my family, job, ministry, etc.
- I couldn't hurt my adultery partner by breaking it off. It would be cruel. They might commit suicide.
- What would I reward myself with when I've done something good? Lust is what I want.
- It is easier to retreat to lust when I've been hurt. It understands me and cares for me.
- I've tried this before, and sex is everywhere. I don't have a chance, so why try and fail again?

If any of these sound like you, you're starting the right journey. These thoughts aren't reasons to quit. They are indicators that you are torn about doing something important. If you resonate with these thoughts, they reveal that this *False Love* journey will meet you where you are.

Because you've felt the weight of shame and social stigma about your choices, it is important for you to know that *every decision in this study is yours to make or not make.* Like it or not, for better or worse, the direction of your life is in your hands. This study will not attempt to compel you to do things you don't want to do.

You will be asked to honestly examine the role and impact of sexual sin in your life. Where you have dishonored the primary relationships in your life—such as your relationship with God and current or future spouse—you will be encouraged to pursue sexual integrity through humble, honest reliance on God with the support of those at G4. That is our encouragement to you, but the choice is yours.

> ▶ **Reflection:*** What would you be giving up if you relinquished your sexual sin, broke off your extramarital relationship, or quit viewing pornography? This is an important and often neglected question. Change comes with a cost. It is important to put that cost into words now so that you do not view it as a legitimate excuse to quit later.

Be honest about your answer to this question. You may not like what you write. You might be ashamed to let someone else read it. Or you may be defensive because you believe no one will give your answer the weight it deserves. But if you are going to seriously consider changing, then you need to assess (a) what you will be forsaking and (b) what needs to be replaced through God-honoring relationships. Avoiding this question—or being superficial in your reflection—is an excellent way to sabotage your progress on this journey.

ASSESSING YOUR LEVEL OF MOTIVATION

The pattern of changing any unwanted but enjoyable behavior is captured in the following sentiment: "Quitting smoking is easy. I've done it a couple dozen times." We want to change, but we don't want to change. We're motivated, but we're not motivated. We think we should change, but we wish people would just leave us alone. This mindset is called *ambivalence*—feeling two contradictory emotions about the same thing. We're good at ambivalence, even if we don't name it.

> ▶ **Read James 1:5–8.** We often see these verses as just a guilt passage. We read it and think, *If this applies to me, I should feel really bad. God must be mad at me.* Start with verse 5 and realize the passage begins by presenting God as generous. God is not upset

---

* It is recommended that you keep a notebook or journal with this book. *False Love* is not a book you just read. To be effective you will need to study, reflect, journal, and discuss what you are learning. Give this journey the time it needs. Allow it to become a memoir of how you regained your life by the grace of God. Writing out answers to the reflections and Bible studies will also help you participate more effectively in your G4 group meetings.

about supplying what we need in our double-minded moments. This will help us trust that there is hope for our fickle desire to change (v. 6). God won't change us against our will. Not receiving anything from God as long as we are double-minded also means God refrains from imposing himself on us (v. 7). Instead, he is loving and warns us against the dangers of our double-minded tendency. At this stage in your journey, you're just starting to get comfortable admitting what God already knows. There is hope because God is not surprised even if we are surprised when we admit how bad things have gotten. Hope begins where you are, and God will always join you there.

> Hope begins where you are, and God will always join you there.

You need to name this tendency toward ambivalence early in your journey. Don't feel ashamed of your conflicted motives. God already knows about them, and he still wants to help. The only people you can lie to are yourself and those who love you. In this section, you will look at five stages of motivation to change from Carlo DiClemente in *Addiction and Change*. These stages are (a) pre-contemplation, (b) contemplation, (c) preparation, (d) action, and (e) maintenance.[1]

It may feel odd for you to hear an addiction resource being used. Are we already declaring that you are a sex addict? No. But addiction paradigms are helpful whenever a set of behaviors have been hidden for an extended time and repeated even when we know our actions will have harmful consequences. That is why we reference this material early in this journey.

Let's look at each of these stages along with how they correlate with the 9-step journey of this study and a general overview of each stage:

1. **Pre-Contemplation** is often completed before you start G4: This is the stage when you didn't anticipate making any changes because you didn't think change was needed. You were probably offended if someone suggested that you needed to change.

2. **Contemplation** is Step 1. Now you are beginning to believe that change might be beneficial and you are wondering what the

process might look like. You are trying to decide whether change is possible, and, if so, whether it is worth it. You want to know what would be required and whether these sacrifices would produce a more satisfying life than continuing with your sexual sin.

3. **Preparation** is Steps 2–4. In this phase you embrace the reality that change is needed. You gather the information necessary to enact an effective and sustainable plan. You assess obstacles, both logistical (external) and motivational (internal). You begin to enlist people to come alongside you for the journey.

4. **Action** is Steps 5–7. Now plans come to life; ideas become choices. Progress is made, and you navigate setbacks. There are successes and failures, but the trajectory of your journey is forward. Techniques become habits, and habits become a lifestyle. The roles once filled by your sexual sin are now filled with healthier, God-honoring ways of managing life.

5. **Maintenance** is Steps 8–9. You embrace a new lifestyle. Increasingly your emotions and thought patterns conform to this new lifestyle. Sexual sin is no longer your reward or escape of choice, and you are enjoying life. At this stage, you begin the work of restoring relationships and pursuing interests that were damaged by your sin.

Although we've presented these stages as corresponding to the 9 steps of G4, stages of motivation are not linear. It's common for people to jump between stages during their journey. For example, you may feel strong motivation to change on Monday (action) but fall on Friday and wonder if the journey is even worth it (contemplation). The goal is not to move in a straight line from one stage to the next, but to realize that no matter where you are in the process, the Lord is there and willing to help you.

▶ **Exercise:** In the margin beside these five levels of motivation write "today" beside where your motivation is now. Write significant dates or events in the margin that come to mind when you read each description. This may not be your first attempt at this journey. Recognizing where you will begin to cover new motivational terrain is important. Realize that every relapse is an opportunity to learn. There is no shame in falling; only quitting.

Your goal at this point is to become more self-aware of your motivation to change. You want to be aware when your motivation fluctuates. It will. Growth in awareness allows you to grow in honesty with others. Honesty with self, God, and others is foundational to change. Everything at G4 is built around this honesty.

> There is no shame in falling; only quitting.

G4 GROUP DISCUSSION: STEP 1, PART ONE

As you discuss this material in G4 group, these questions are meant to facilitate a more honest and beneficial dialogue about this material. Anyone is free to respond to whichever questions they choose.

Experienced Members

- What do you remember about the pre-contemplation and contemplation phases of your journey?
- What factors or experiences were influential in your choice to embrace the pursuit of change?

New Members

- What brings you to G4? How much of your story are you willing to share?
- What is the thing about your sexual sin you most dread giving up?
- How can we pray for you?

Everyone

- What mental or emotional habits indicate you're regressing to a pre-contemplation phase?
- How does it feel to study James 1 and realize you don't have to be defensive about being double-minded?
- Have you experienced a significant setback or victory since last meeting that you should tell the group?

STEP 1
PART TWO

HOW SEVERE IS MY STRUGGLE?

The video for this part of Step 1 can be found at: bradhambrick.com/falselove1p2.

The primary virtue required to complete Step 1 is courage—the courage to engage with questions and challenges we've grown too comfortable avoiding. If you feel a reflex to retreat, withdraw, or hide as you work through this material, be honest about it. Courage doesn't mean the absence of internal resistance. Courage means we're honest about the internal resistance we feel as we continue toward healthy, God-honoring goal despite that resistance.

In this part of Step 1, you are going to be asked to consider what you've long debated. The question is, "How severe is my sexual sin? How ingrained has it become?" As much as possible, we would like you to engage this question objectively. Try to resist allowing defensiveness from previous conversations or arguments to bias your answers. Thank you again for your courage as you try to do this as accurately as possible.

SEXUAL SIN ASSESSMENT

Instructions: Read the following descriptive statements. Mark the answer that most accurately describes your behaviors when they were at their worst. Items with the statement "if married" should also be applied to an engagement or serious dating relationship where faithfulness and exclusivity are reasonable expectations.

(N) almost never, (R) rarely, (S) sometimes, (F) frequently, or (A) almost always

1. In my mind, I rate people based upon my assessment of their attractiveness.	N R S F A
2. I ignore or think less of people I find unattractive.	N R S F A
3. With couples, I compare the man and woman to see who "married up."	N R S F A
4. When I'm attracted to someone, I want to make them "mine" (ownership).	N R S F A
5. I would break up with someone I found less attractive for someone more attractive.	N R S F A
6. I take more than a glance at an attractive person who is not my spouse.	N R S F A
7. I have preferred features I observe, compare, and "score" in other people.	N R S F A
8. I look for places and times to catch revealing glimpses of people I find attractive.	N R S F A
9. I keep watching sexual advertisements or commercials.	N R S F A
10. I go out of my way to be around people I find attractive or romantically stimulating.	N R S F A
11. I imagine people are romantically interested in me after a conversation.	N R S F A
12. I am preoccupied with sexual thoughts or self-made romantic narratives.	N R S F A
13. I place myself in the romantic plots of books, movies, or pornography.	N R S F A
14. I am often disappointed in real relationships.	N R S F A
15. I use romantic fantasy to escape stressful situations.	N R S F A
16. I watch television shows I know will have scantily clad actors or actresses.	N R S F A
17. I search for arousing images in magazines or advertisements.	N R S F A
18. I visit websites with nude images or sexual stories.	N R S F A

19. I have preferred sexual websites I visit regularly.   N R S F A

20. I have developed a preference for specific types of   N R S F A
sexual content or stories.

21. I visit chat rooms to talk with people I do not   N R S F A
know about sex.

22. I use direct messaging in social media to have   N R S F A
sexual conversations.

23. I engage in sexting or live online chats for sexual   N R S F A
conversation.

24. I have posted my personal information on dating   N R S F A
websites.

25. I have visited a strip club.   N R S F A

26. [If married] I keep conversations with my oppo-   N R S F A
site sex "friend" secret.

27. [If married] I put more forethought into conversa-   N R S F A
tions with my opposite sex "friend" than my spouse.

28. [If married] I have private channels of communi-   N R S F A
cation with my opposite sex "friend" that my spouse
doesn't know about.

29. [If married] Conversations with my opposite sex   N R S F A
"friend" are flirty and have sexual overtones.

30. [If married] I hold hands, give tight hugs, or kiss   N R S F A
my opposite sex "friend."

31. I have attended events or places knowingly pursu-   N R S F A
ing sex.

32. I have proposed having sex with someone and   N R S F A
have been turned down.

33. I have put my personal information on a website   N R S F A
looking for a sex partner.

34. I have had a onetime sexual encounter with   N R S F A
someone who is not my spouse.

35. I have had multiple onetime sexual encounters.   N R S F A

36. I am in a sexually active relationship with some-   N R S F A
one other than my spouse.

37. I am hiding expenses that I've incurred while courting this relationship.	N R S F A
38. I am pulling away from friends who would disapprove of my adultery.	N R S F A
39. The sex in my adulterous relationship is an expression of genuine affection.	N R S F A
40. I overtly express "I love you" to my adultery partner.	N R S F A
41. My adultery partner and I have discussed leaving our spouses for each other.	N R S F A
42. I resent my spouse for being the reason I am not with my adultery partner.	N R S F A
43. I have researched the possibility of divorce.	N R S F A
44. I have thought about when and how to tell my spouse or kids I'm leaving.	N R S F A
45. I view myself as belonging to my adultery partner more than my spouse.	N R S F A
46. I have forced another adult to have sex against their will.	N R S F A
47. I have touched or initiated a minor touching me sexually.	N R S F A
48. As an adult, I have had sex with a minor.	N R S F A
49. I have viewed child pornography.	N R S F A
50. I struggle with same-sex attraction.	N R S F A

Scoring Key: Each criterion is assessed with five questions and should be scored as indicated below:

"N" and "R" response = 0 points
"S" response = 1 point
"F" response = 2 points
"A" response = 3 points

If your total score is 5 to 9, it is a significant concern.
If your total score is 10 or higher, it is a life-dominating struggle.

As you review the findings from this evaluation, you will notice that it is built around a progression from objectifying people to (if married) being more committed to your adultery partner than your spouse. **However, this progression is not meant to imply that this is an absolute or inevitable unfolding cycle.** Some adultery does not begin with pornography. Pornography does not necessarily lead to adultery. The purpose of the progression is to help you see more clearly why Jesus would teach that looking at someone with "lustful intent" is a form of or seed for adultery (Matthew 5:21–30). While the progression is not an inevitable slippery slope, reading the descriptions of the full journey into lustful depravity should sober you about your sin. Figure 1 provides a visual of the "small steps" between lust and adultery.

1. **Objectifying a person:** Reducing people to a set of appealing features and measuring people's value by how much they please you.
2. **Public visual lust:** Using the objectification above as a scoring system for actual people.
3. **Private narrative lust:** Allowing the scoring system to develop into a story in which you interact with someone romantically in your imagination.
4. **Pornography:** Using print, television, or internet to provide more "choice" objects of lust. Pursuing nude images and videos and having the imagination expanded by professional "storytellers."
5. **Interaction with a real, anonymous person:** The other participant in the story becomes a real person with a real voice and a free will.
6. **Emotional affair:** This is an emotionally enmeshed relationship with a real person that may involve kissing, caressing, fondling, and other non-intercourse affections.
7. **One-time sexual affair:** Now the intercourse barrier has been crossed, but (as in the case of a prostitute or drunken business trip fling) the relational connection may be low.
8. **Affair in a committed relationship:** In terms of marital threat, the sexual affair is now secondary to the deepening "love" between the spouse and adultery partner. Sex is no longer a mere expression of passion but also devotion.
9. **Affair as a pseudo-spouse/leaving:** No longer is the faithful spouse making the decision regarding divorce. The unfaithful spouse is the active party seeking to dissolve the marriage to pursue their adultery partner.

Figure 2. The Journey from Lust to Adultery

▶ **Read Matthew 5:21–30.** In this passage Jesus deals with two sins—anger and lust—in the same way: He identifies the heart issue, warns against the full-grown sin, and calls for radical action to remove that sin. If your instinct is to argue that people should not face prison time for common anger, you are both right and missing Jesus's point. Jesus is warning you, not advocating for legislation. Jesus is saying, "Take whatever steps are necessary to remove lust from your life. Unless your excuse for not changing is of greater consequence than losing an eye or hand, it is just that—an excuse." Don't allow a pattern of behavior to persist in your life if it is one that will destroy your life and hurt those you love. Jesus's warning to you is motivated by love, not anger. He doesn't want to see you continue living in bondage to sexual sin. He wants you to be free.

- Statements 1–5:   (Total: _____ in 5 questions)

  These statements describe sexual sin expressed through **objectifying people**. A person is more than a body. A person is more than a source of visual or emotional pleasure. Lust begins by removing the soul and personhood from the people we find attractive. The possibility of an authentic relationship is reduced when we determine people's value based on their appearance.

  ▶ **Reflection:** What aspects of a person (i.e., figure, personality, intelligence, wealth, power) do you most highly value (i.e., "grade")? How has this led to unhealthy relationships or unwise choices? How has this led to insecurity in your life?

- Statements 6–10:   (Total: _____ in 5 questions)

  These statements describe sexual sin expressed through **public visual lust**. Lust happens when we use the lens of objectification to evaluate people. Lust is both a visual activity (i.e., staring, ogling) and a social activity (i.e., elevating or devaluing). Lust is not the act of merely noticing an attractive person; it is giving more value to someone we deem appealing than to someone we deem unappealing.

  ▶ **Reflection:** How, when, and where does the visual activity of your public visual lust express itself? That is, when do you need to be more disciplined with your eyes? How, when, and where does the social activity of your public visual lust express itself? That is, when do you give preferential treatment to people you deem more appealing?

- Statements 11–15:   (Total: _____ in 5 questions)

  These statements describe sexual sin expressed through **private narrative lust**. With lust, the story (i.e., being strong, being desirable, being rescued, etc.) can be more intoxicating than the visual appeal. This is why romance movies and pornography use these themes in their plot development. In this sense, lust is an escape from reality. We begin to tell ourselves untrue, unrealistic stories of romance and pleasure and get lost in them.

  > Jesus's warning to you is motivated by love, not anger. He wants you to be free.

  ► **Reflection:** What are the most common themes of your narrative lusts? How does entertaining these themes increase your dissatisfaction with real life and real people?

- Statements 16–20:   (Total: _____ in 5 questions)

  These statements describe sexual sin expressed through **pornography**. Now both professional actors and professional storytellers are involved in bringing your romantic or sexual fantasies to life. This stretches your lust-based imagination and adds the sense that you are a connoisseur of something excellent rather than a participant in something that dishonors those you claim to be relishing.

  ► **Reflection:** How have your expectations of relationships or a romantic partner changed as you've viewed pornography? What common situations in your life have become unhealthily associated with romance or sexuality?

- Statements 21–25:   (Total: _____ in 5 questions)

  These statements describe sexual sin expressed with **a real but anonymous person**. Now the object of lust (rarely viewed as a real person with a soul) has a mind and will of their own. They still have a vested interest in pleasing you (e.g., financial reasons or seeking companionship), but it is not a prerecorded scene and, therefore, gives the facade of a real relationship.

  ► **Reflection:** How has commercialized romantic or sexual interaction impacted your satisfaction with real relationships? How has the "courage" anonymity provided increased your timidity in real relationships?

- Statements 26–30:   (Total: _____ in 5 questions)

  These statements describe sexual sin expressed through an **emotional affair**. Now you know the other person and they know you. Your sexual sin is becoming bolder and taking more risks to find its fulfillment. Risk adds to the stimulation of sexual sin and becomes a false standard by which real relationships and sex are measured.

  ▶ **Reflection:** What social risks are you taking that would have previously scared you? How does taking these risks make an honoring relationship—one without the risks of getting caught—feel less satisfying?

- Statements 31–35:   (Total: _____ in 5 questions)

  These statements describe sexual sin expressed through a **one-time sexual encounter**. There is no longer a line you pretend you won't cross. This sexual sin is not part of a committed relationship, but purely a matter of self-gratification. Even if the other person is using you for the same self-gratification, this type of sexual encounter is stripping sex of the bonding impact God intended to provide for a husband and wife.

  ▶ **Reflection:** How does "casualizing" sex impact future dating relationships that might lead toward marriage? How does your willingness to expose your spouse (or future spouse) to a risk for STDs devalue that relationship?

- Statements 36–40:   (Total: _____ in 5 questions)

  These statements describe sexual sin expressed through an **affair in a committed relationship**. Sex now means something to you. You can no longer hide behind the lie that "it's only sex" (which was never true). Ending the sin now feels like it would require "closure," which is a noble word for relapse. If the onetime sexual encounter reduced the bonding impact of sex, this expression bonds you to someone other than your spouse.

  ▶ **Reflection:** How has your adultery partner changed the way you think about your spouse (if married)? What do you criticize in your spouse and praise in your adultery partner to justify your actions?

- Statements 41–45:   (Total: _____ in 5 questions)

  These statements describe sexual sin expressed through an **affair with a pseudo-spouse**. You are no longer thinking about how to tell your spouse the truth and wondering if they will take you back. You're trying to figure out how to tell your spouse it's over and wondering what your new life will be like. If you have children, do not fall into the trap of expecting more of their resilience than your integrity by assuming your children adapt to whatever ways your sin damages their home of origin.

  > ▶ **Reflection:** How has your happiness trumped the well-being of anyone else in your life? Do you really believe the lie that "nobody in your life can be happy unless you're happy"? That mindset will also destroy any of the happily-ever-after stories you're telling yourself about this new relationship.

- Statements 46–50:   (These statements do not score together.)

  These statements describe **expressions of sexual sin not addressed in *False Love***. *False Love* is a curriculum for sexual sins that have been reinforced through habituation and cultivated through entertaining lusts. *False Love* is not a curriculum designed to replace the consequences for **immoral activity that is also illegal as in responses 46–49**.

  - If the actions that have led you to this *False Love* study or a G4 group are also illegal, you are encouraged to self-report to the appropriate authorities. When you have committed an illegal action against another person, this is what it means to love your neighbor as yourself (Mark 12:30–31).
  - Members of your G4 group are not expected to keep illegal sexual activity confidential. The responsibility of G4 members to you does not usurp their responsibility as citizens toward those you harmed.
  - There is forgiveness and hope for change, but it begins with admitting your actions to the civil authority God has given to protect the innocent.

  False Love is not a curriculum designed for **unwanted same-sex attraction (as in response 50)**.

- To categorize unwanted same-sex attraction as sexual addiction is inaccurate. Most same-sex attraction is not the result of a deepening struggle with pornography and lust.
- If your unwanted same-sex attraction has been reinforced through habituated sexual activity and thought, then *False Love* and G4 can be useful tools in fighting against these habituated expressions of lust.
- Currently, the best Christian resources we are aware of to support someone with unwanted same-sex attraction can be found at The Sexual and Gender Identity Institute led by Dr. Mark Yarhouse.[1]

A BRIEF WORD ON SEXUAL ADDICTION

Am I a sex addict? Can you be addicted to an activity as you can a substance? If my sexual sin has become an addiction, would that make it less sinful? In a study like *False Love*, these are questions we need to engage. Views vary on behavioral addictions (highly habituated activities like gambling or immoral sex). Many of the books referenced in this study use the language of addiction. We reference these books because they bring valuable insight into the description and assessment of sexual sin struggles. We do not believe you have to embrace the language of being a sex addict to benefit from this study.

If you wonder whether your sexual sin has an addictive quality, answer the ten questions below. The more items you mark yes, the more life-dominating your sexual sin has become, and the more accurate the term *addiction* may be.

Yes	No	You repeatedly fail to resist sexual impulses.
Yes	No	You give increasing time to sexual sin.
Yes	No	You have been unsuccessful in efforts to stop, reduce, or control your sexual sin.
Yes	No	You are pursuing deeper and more depraved sexual themes.
Yes	No	You are preoccupied with sex, sexual behavior, or sexual humor.
Yes	No	You engage in sexual behavior even when it interferes with job, school, or social expectations.

Yes   No   You continue sexual behavior when it negatively
             impacts your marriage, emotional, or spiritual life.
Yes   No   You notice an increase in intensity, frequency,
             depravity, or risk is necessary to for the desired effect.
Yes   No   You sacrifice recreational or other healthy outlets to
             engage in sexual release or relationship.
Yes   No   You experience distress, anxiety, restlessness, or
             irritability if unable to engage in the behavior.

CONCLUSION

This is always a hard section to complete. You don't yet have to be confident in all your answers at this point in your G4 journey. But you do need to be humble enough to resist becoming defensive and courageous enough to want to know accurate answers. Remember, reading a section is not the same thing as completing a step. Early in our journeys, we need to be reminded of this often.

> Realize that courage comes before change, and while courage often feels uncomfortable, but it pursues sexual integrity to honor God regardless of discomfort.

Your goal at this stage is simply to consider each question and desire to know the truth more than you fear the truth being known. If you do that, you've done something very significant. Realize that courage comes before change, and while courage often feels uncomfortable, but it pursues sexual integrity to honor God regardless of discomfort.

G4 GROUP DISCUSSION: STEP 1, PART TWO

As you discuss this material in G4 group, these questions are meant to facilitate a more honest and beneficial dialogue about this material. Anyone is free to respond to whichever questions they choose.

Experienced Members

- What things do you look back and remember felt "really important" that were actually more of a distraction than a benefit?

- How important was it for you personally to decide whether the term *addiction* was a good description of your sexual sin? (Answers may vary in the group.)

New Members

- Which questions in this assessment were most difficult for you to answer objectively?
- What did you learn about yourself and the experience of addiction from completing the assessment?
- How can we pray for you?

Everyone

- What is your biggest internal obstacle to admitting the depth of your struggle?
- In what areas of your life have you been tempted to regress back toward thinking that continued self-destructive behavior seems easier and more appealing than healthy living?
- Have you experienced a significant setback or victory since last meeting that you should tell the group?

STEP 1
PART THREE

BOTH LUST AND LYING

The video for this part of Step 1 can be found at: bradhambrick.com/falselove1p3.

If this entire journey could be reduced to a single step, it would be this—*be honest.* Honesty may be more difficult than abstaining from sexual sin. At the risk of offending you, you can't get trapped in sexual sin without being a good liar. You won't get far enough into the process if you can't cover your tracks. That's why honesty is the number one "technique" to emancipate yourself from sexual sin.

> If this entire journey could be reduced to a single step, it would be this— *be honest.*

The most dangerous lies are the ones you believe. The first person you need to be honest with is yourself. When you believe your own lies, they cripple your motivation to change and become more convincing as you tell them to others. Consider these quotes:

> When lies become your native language, you are in trouble. . . . The more lies you've told . . . the more lies you believe. —Ed Welch[1]

> I was beginning to realize that my problems were not just sexual but revolved around a lifestyle of lying and deceit. Up until this time, had I been asked if I was a liar, I would have been offended and would have answered with an emphatic "No!" Sadly, I would have believed I was telling the truth. —Earl and Sandy Wilson[2]

Memorize this statement: *You will never be more free than you are honest.*

> ▶ **Read Numbers 32:23; Job 34:21; Proverbs 15:3; Luke 8:17; and Hebrews 4:13.** You may have already experienced the truth contained in these verses. We lie because we believe we can control the truth by the stories we tell and the information we give or withhold. We begin to believe we are larger than the truth, rather than believing that truth is the reality in which we live. We can no more control truth than we can control the wind. Remind yourself regularly that honesty is not optional; the only thing we can choose is whether we are voluntarily or involuntarily honest. Truth will be known. Pause and pray again for the courage to be honest because truth-speaking and sexual integrity are also two sides of the same coin.

In many ways, this section may be the hardest part of this entire journey. It will be hard for at least two reasons: First, it will require you to abandon lying and deception as your primary tactic for hiding your sin. Second, it will require you to be honest with yourself about *how* you've been dishonest—not just *what* you've misrepresented.

FRAGMENTATION

One way to think of deception is fragmentation—telling parts or fragments of your story as if they were the whole story and expecting others to respond accordingly. This is what we do when we ask a friend to hold us accountable but get defensive when they press us with questions we don't want to answer by saying something like, "I thought you were my friend. I can't believe you would be judgmental and think so poorly of me." We give them part of our story, expect them to trust that it's the whole story, and get offended when they don't.

TWELVE WAYS WE DECEIVE OTHERS

1. **Omitted facts.** The story you tell is true and there are no false statements in it. However, the most relevant information concerning sexual integrity is omitted. For example, telling what you did all day and omitting the forty-five minutes you met up with your

adultery partner, or talking about the work you accomplished on the computer and leaving out the time you spent looking at pornography. The fact that your lies are within a true story and hard to verify gives you the false impression that you can control whether the full truth is ever known.

As a rule, if there is a question you hope is not asked, then you should voluntarily disclose the answer. People should not have to ask the right question to get the needed information to help. That is the equivalent of a patient lying to their doctor about where it hurts because he didn't specifically ask, "Are you having chest pains?"

> ▶ **Reflection:** How do you lie by omitted or altered facts, and what are the most recent or significant examples?

2. **False facts.** This is a step beyond omitting facts. The story may be true, but elements of the story are false. For example, while explaining why you were not home when expected, you make up a traffic accident that delayed you by an hour. To explain the virus or pop-ups on the computer, you make up a story about letting your coworker borrow your laptop.

    If anything you say is false, then everything you've said is self-destructive. We never lie to cover up the things that make our life better. We only lie when what we've done is offensive to others or destructive to ourselves.

    > ▶ **Reflection:** How do you lie by false facts, and what are the most recent or significant examples?

3. **False emotion.** Now you must play the part. If your lies are true, then they would result in certain emotions. If you are going to remain "free," then you must become an actor. When we feign emotions to protect our sin, the "audience" does not know they're watching a "show." This makes our deception even more destructive to the relationship because now our loved one realizes that not just our words—but also our emotions—were a performance. Tim Chester gives a common example of what this type of lying looks like, and though he is speaking to a husband, it applies to anyone in a committed relationship.

> The secret that you hide from your wife [or husband] will create a barrier in your relationship. You may criticize her in order to feel better about your own shortcomings. You will distance yourself from her to avoid any chance of exposure. . . . In some cases you may even pick a fight or find fault with your wife, to justify your porn use.[3]

Lying by false emotions is the best way to teach people to mistrust you. When people doubt both our words and emotions, they lose faith in anything we say, unless they see direct evidence to the contrary.

> ▶ **Reflection:** How do you lie by false emotions, and what are the most recent or significant examples?

4.   **False story.** False facts produce false emotions. Together they require a false story. Your lies begin to create their own world in which they could be true. Your spouse asks if you're being unfaithful, and you feign being upset that they would even have to ask that question. You follow up with concern, knowing that concern hides your sin because you know that is not the characteristic of an unfaithful spouse. You are creating the false story of being a highly concerned spouse; you are covering your sin with the façade of concern. You try to live between reality and your false story. Reality won't bend, and your lies can't break without you being found out. You and those around you are forced to live stretched between these two worlds.

Telling the truth now means more than correcting facts. Initially, this form of lying feels the most powerful because you're playing a godlike role. Acknowledging this type of lying is the most shameful because we realize how much we have manipulated everyone around us.

> ▶ **Reflection:** How do you lie by false story, and what are the most recent or significant examples?

5.   **Minimizing.** Maybe you are smart enough to avoid the false route. Maybe you can see how that would inevitably blow up in your face.

Instead, you choose a more strategic route. You don't change the facts, but merely change the significance of those facts. Minimizing is one of the more popular methods of lying. For example, you talk about it being "just porn" or you and your adultery partner being "just friends."

You should not weigh any sexual behavior until it's been fully disclosed to someone acquainted with your struggle. Find someone who knows you well and is committed to your integrity. They can help you determine the severity of a setback. Avoid language that sizes a concern as small (a "slip," "mishap," "mistake," etc.).

> Lying by false emotions is the best way to teach people to mistrust you.

▶ **Reflection:** How do you lie by minimizing, and what are the most recent or significant examples? What phrases do you use to minimize?

6. **Blame-shifting.** Maybe you accept the facts and admit how serious the problem is, but you lie by shifting the responsibility: "It's true and it's bad, but it's not my fault." For sexual sin, there are several common targets for blame-shifting.

   • **My needs**—This is the common pop-psychology blame-shifting method that is even endorsed by many popular Christian authors. For example, that's just how men/women are. I had to fill my "love tank" somehow.

   > No one deserves sin. Sin is not something to be deserved or desired, but is something to avoid at all cost. —Steve Gallagher[4]

   > In our culture sex is everything and sex is nothing. . . . One of the things that porn does is to make us think marriage is for sex. But it's the other way round: sex is for marriage. . . . So what is sex for? It is, first and foremost, an act of unification, uniting two people into one flesh. . . . That's why porn—along with all sex outside of marriage—is a sham, a fiction, a lie. You can no more "try out" sex than you can "try out" birth. The

very act produces a new reality that cannot be undone.
—Tim Chester[5]

- **My spouse**—This is often paired with "needs" language. This can be summarized by the statement, "If my spouse treated me the way I wanted to be treated, I would not sin." The responsibility for honoring God is shifted from self to spouse.

> The offending spouse sometimes blames the mate or a deteriorating marriage for the affair. Poor companionship and a lack of lovemaking make a couple more vulnerable, but there is still a choice. If you leave the keys in your car and someone steals it, it is still the thief's fault. The adulterer chose to have the affair. —Doug Rosenau[6]

- **My history/personality**—Sexual sin may be influenced by early sexualization, a history of sexual abuse, or personality factors such as compulsivity. But to assign responsibility for your sin to these factors is a deceptive form of blame-shifting.
- **"It just happened"**—No, it didn't. Sin requires a sinner, just as fishing requires a fisherman. For many this is an appealing form of blame-shifting because it allows everyone to be innocent.
- **"I was seduced"**—We are seduced because we want to be seduced. People fall for get-rich-quick schemes because they want to be rich. In a marriage, this blame-shifting tactic can be appealing because it allows you and your spouse to be "on the same team" against the other person. The adultery partner is equally to blame, but if healthy restoration is to occur, they cannot be blamed for your behavior.

As a rule, explanation comes after ownership. If you are trying to explain why something happened before fully owning your choices, you are blame-shifting.

> ▶ **Reflection:** How do you lie by blame-shifting, and what are the most recent or significant examples? Who or what are your most common targets for blame-shifting?

7. **"I don't know."** It is legal to plead the Fifth in a courtroom, but it is deceitful in recovery. The statement "I don't know" is often

used to buy time while preparing to do a better job at another form of lying. "I don't know" is also used to force the questioner to nag or badger so their action can become the focal point of the conversation.

If you know the answer but are not proud of it, share it anyway. If you are tempted to blame-shift, be honest about it. For instance, "Right now I'm having a hard time answering your question because I can tell I want to blame others." If you are genuinely uncertain, answer as clearly as you can and acknowledge the incompleteness of your answer. For instance, "I know this won't completely answer the question you've asked, but here is what I can explain about my actions . . ."

> ►Reflection: How do you lie by saying "I don't know," and what are the most recent or significant examples?

8. **Hidden agenda.** This is deception by setup. For example: You do something nice for your spouse so that you feel less guilty (without having to repent or change) and (intentionally or not) your spouse feels guilty for addressing the sin in your life. Self-pity is another common form of deception by hidden agenda. The essence of self-pity is beating yourself up over your sin instead of embracing repentance and change. The effect is that your sorrow becomes a guilt shield against the hard work of engaging change or speaking words of timely truth.

> ►Reflection: How have you lied about your sexual sin by hidden agenda, and what are the most recent or significant examples?

9. **Verbalizing suspicion.** This is deception by counterattack. When you confront me in my sin, I attack you for your sins (real or fabricated). If I can't prove my case, then I will try to change who is on trial. An example is asking questions like "Can you tell me you've never been attracted to somebody else?" or "I don't ask you about your credit card. Why are you asking me about mine? Can I have the password to your email accounts too?"

► **Reflection:** How have you lied about your sexual sin by verbalizing suspicion, and what are the most recent or significant examples?

10. **Late truth.** Post-discovery confession is not honesty. Often, we want points for admitting what people already know. When we add the false emotion of being offended that "our best is not good enough" or "I'll never be able to please you," we only compound the situation.

    Expecting trust by merely acknowledging truth that has already been discovered is manipulative. It is like expecting to be paid for someone else's work. Remember, you only earn trust for truth that you voluntarily contribute to the relationship.

    ► **Reflection:** How do you lie by late truth, and what are the most recent or significant examples?

11. **Changing definitions.** Altering the definition of words is one of the most prevalent tactics of manipulation. Be very cautious when you are hinging your defense or request on an emotionally loaded word like "friend," "forgiveness," or "trust." There is a strong probability that you are using these words, intentionally or not, in a manipulative manner.

    ► **Reflection:** How do you lie by changing definitions, and what are the most recent or significant examples?

12. **Exaggeration.** This is deception by magnification. Unlike other forms of lying that seek to shrink or hide the truth, exaggeration makes the truth larger than it really is. Truth moves from being an enemy to being a weapon. For example, "You're right. You and the kids are better off without me because I'm a despicable person. I'll leave and you'll never have to be bothered by me again."

    Exaggeration places the emphasis on your perspective or experience more than the truth. Exaggeration is an attempt to force people to live in your world rather than join them in the real world. It is like self-pity; it tries to force others to rescue us from the consequences of our own choices.

▶ **Reflection:** How do you lie by exaggeration, and what are the most recent or significant examples?

▶ **Read Ecclesiastes 2:1–11.** The book of Ecclesiastes might be called "The Big Book of Step 1." In this book, Solomon admits that he tried everything under the sun to find satisfaction and that it was all ultimately unfulfilling. One of the biggest hindrances to honestly admitting our sin is the belief that we are going to miss out on the good life, or that our sin has made the good life unattainable (so why not go on sinning if life is already inevitably wrecked?), leaving sin seemingly as the best option. These are lies you must put away if you are ever going to put away your sin. God has promised that he came to give us a full life (John 10:10) and that nothing we have done can separate us from that good life because of what Christ did on our behalf (Romans 8:34–39). Doubting either of these truths ultimately keeps people in their sin.

FINAL THOUGHTS ON STEP 1

Now is a pivotal time in your process of change. If you remain alone in your pursuit of sexual integrity, you will likely fail. The most important thing you can do at this point is to involve someone else (preferably multiple people). This is why this curriculum is written to be studied in a G4 group. You need the support and examples that come from walking alongside people on a comparable journey.[7]

To reach the end of this first step is a significant achievement. Well done! It is difficult to wrestle through the number of subjects you've already addressed and to face things you've tried to avoid for some time. Honor the work you have put in to reach this point by continuing to take the next steps toward freedom.

G4 GROUP DISCUSSION: STEP 1, PART THREE

As you discuss this material in G4 group, these questions are meant to facilitate a more honest and beneficial dialogue about this material. Anyone is free to respond to whichever questions they choose.

Experienced Members

- What was hardest to admit in your pattern of deceit?
- How self-aware were you about your deceit when you began to get serious about sexual integrity?

New Members

- How hard is it for you to hear, "You can't get trapped in sexual sin without being a good liar"?
- What patterns of deceit are you most prone to use?
- How can we pray for you?

Everyone

- What has been the clearest example of your blame-shifting regarding your sexual sin?
- Outside of those in G4, who are you currently being honest with?
- Have you experienced a significant setback or victory since the last meeting that you should tell the group?

STEP 2
ACKNOWLEDGE the breadth and impact of my sin.

At the end of this step, I want to be able to say . . .

"I am beginning to see the extent and impact of my sexual sin. It is bigger than I wanted to admit [describe your minimization] and still may be bigger than I realize. Apart from God's grace I would continue to be a person in bondage. I acknowledge that there is no hope and no freedom in minimizing my sin. Before I can truly understand the significance of Jesus in my life, I must acknowledge the magnitude of what he is empowering me to overcome."

STEP 2
PART ONE

THE HISTORY AND GROWTH OF YOUR SIN

The video for this part of Step 2 can be found at: bradhambrick.com/falselove2p1.

T hank you for continuing this journey. It takes courage to persevere in something this difficult. You are to be commended for completing Step 1 and beginning Step 2. In this step, we will examine the breadth and impact of our sexual sin.

In Step 1, we named our struggle. Now we will examine it. Metaphorically speaking, we said "I have a dog" in Step 1. Now, in Step 2, we will assess whether we have a poodle, Labrador retriever, or Great Dane. This is an important advance because it is possible to admit a problem exists while still minimizing its severity. That is something we want to avoid. The reality is that our level of commitment and effort toward change will correspond with how severe we believe our sin is. If we underestimate the problem, we are unlikely to persevere through the process of change.

Unless we acknowledge the breadth and impact of our sexual sin, our efforts at change will be limited to our most overt and recent sins. Omitting Step 2 also results in rooting our efforts at change in the powerful emotions we feel (shame in a bad moment; relief or pride in a good moment). We want to see our sin accurately so that we will respond appropriately and consistently.

> Every Christian . . . who looks at porn wants to stop, but many of us want to stop just a little bit less than we want to keep going. . . . Here's a promise. You will never stop until you begin to see the monstrous nature of the sin you are committing. You will never stop until the sin is more horrifying to you than

38

the commission of the sin is enjoyable. You will need to hate that sin before you can find freedom from it. —Tim Challies[1]

To accomplish the goals of Step 2, we will invite you to examine the following three areas of your life:

- the history and growth of your sin;
- the impact your sin has had on you; and
- the impact your sin has had on others.

Understanding the history and develop-ment of a behavior is an important part of changing it. Often we forget or never notice when and why we began to do something. When this happens, the action feels com-pletely natural and, therefore, its continuation is reinforced through the false notion that this is how things have always been and should be.

> If we underestimate the problem, we are unlikely to persevere through the process of change.

Recognizing how my pattern of sexual obsessions first devel-oped its particular shape helped the tumblers fall into place for me in terms of understanding myself. —Anonymous tes-timony in David Powlison's *Pornography: Slaying the Dragon*[2]

There is another reason for this kind of examination. Consider where most people today learn about sex—movies, internet sites, romance novels, or pornography. These sources teach many (maybe most) people about sex. What do these sources have in common? They are industries designed to create an appetite for their product.

Likewise, if you learned about nutrition from a baker who sold cheesecakes, your understanding of a healthy diet would probably be distorted. Therefore, we need to examine our history to identify not only when we began doing harmful things, but when we began believ-ing inaccurate or distorted things about sex. Learning the history of our false beliefs helps us root sexually pure behaviors in a godly under-standing of sexuality.

There is a caution as we engage Step 2. While overcoming sexual sin, it is easy to begin to view your sexuality as evil or as your enemy. It is not. God created us as sexual beings and declared sexuality good

(Genesis 1:26–31). We do not want your G4 journey to lead you to believe that sexual desires are inherently bad. That would be the equivalent of someone who struggles with pride believing that confidence was sinful.

TRACING THE HISTORY OF YOUR SIN

We return to the progression of sexual sin you worked through in the assessment of Step 1. With each stage in the progression, we will provide questions to allow you to write a chronological history of your battle with sexual sin. Write your answers on separate paper. Leave room for questions raised by your counselor, accountability partner, or spouse. Be honest. Retreating to lies or partial truths at this point destroys everything you are working toward.

If you are married, this exercise should be used as the basis for your **full disclosure.** You should discuss with your spouse when and how they would like to receive this full disclosure. As hard as it will be for you to share, it will be at least equally hard for your spouse to hear. For that reason, you should defer to what allows your spouse to feel most secure during this time. You and your spouse should also plan for what each of you will do immediately after the full disclosure because that will likely be an emotionally intense time for each of you.

Your full disclosure in Step 2 can easily be confused with the confession you will be asked to do in Step 5. At this time, you are merely telling your spouse a full and accurate history of your sin, which is also part of their history since they became one with you in marriage. When we conflate Step 2 and Step 5, we rush our spouse. We create the expectation that immediately upon learning of our sin they should be ready to process that history and respond with grace.

> I recommend a two-stage confession: An initial, honest disclosure of the facts, followed by a reflective, thorough, God-centered confession. This approach recognizes the importance of an immediate acknowledgement to your spouse and pastor or counselor. It also recognizes that a more thorough and careful repentance is needed. . . . Come clean completely. [Your spouse] may or may not forgive you. But if she later discovers you have held back or minimized important facts, the odds of

her forgiving and trusting you severely diminish. If the adultery itself does not end the marriage, your half-truths may kill it. —Robert D. Jones[3]

A full disclosure is not sharing graphic or sordid details about your sexual activity. But avoiding graphic details is not a reason to leave out information about your sin. Do not fall into the trap of believing that it is noble to leave out details to protect your spouse from pain. That is not protection; it is deceit.

An issue most people struggle with is the advisability of confessing undiscovered affairs, both past and present. Confession is vital in restoring honesty and rebuilding trust. . . . Treating your mate as fragile or fearing conflict are inadequate reasons for not confessing. —Doug Rosenau[4]

▶ **Read Proverbs 12:13–28.** Before you begin writing your full disclosure, consider this passage that contrasts a life of honesty with a life of deceit. The honesty and transparency of your full disclosure are the difference between peace and despair, joy and misery, life and death. You will likely be tempted to think that further deception and concealment is the only way you will know peace, joy, and life. But listen to God tell you that is a lie in Proverbs 12 (v. 15). If you want to build enduring relationships, speak truth; if you want your world to continue crumbling, hide the truth (v. 18). The Lord will delight in you if you are honest, even if that honesty is the confession of sin (v. 22). Continued deceit will weigh you down with anxiety, but confession is the first step to joy (v. 25). You have been headed toward death, but honesty is the path to life (v. 28). Remind yourself of these things frequently as you work on your disclosure.

Questions to Consider for a Full Disclosure

You can be fully honest without being vivid. The questions provided below are worded to help you do this.

- **Objectifying people.** When did you first begin classifying people by favorable–unfavorable physical features or personal traits? How did you begin to arrange your life to pursue or be liked by these "better" people? How did these changes in your social life result in more shallow or disingenuous relationships? Did you evaluate yourself as being high (pride) or low (shame) on your own objectification scale?

- **Public visual lust.** What features (i.e., appearance) or qualities (i.e., charisma, intelligence, humor) are you most prone to notice and linger on? What locations or activities are (present sin) or have been (past sin) the most frequent or concentrated sources of visual temptation? How have you arranged your life to feed your appetite for public visual lust?

- **Private narrative lust.** What themes repeat most in your private narrative lust? What insecurities are calmed or desires met through these themes? What movies or books best capture the themes of your private narrative lusts? How much time do you spend in private fantasy about these themes?

- **Pornography.** What was your first exposure to pornography? What parts of everyday life or conversation do you sexualize to the point of becoming pornographic? What rituals do you use as you prepare to participate in pornography?

> Sexual addiction seems unmanageable because acting out seems to just "happen." Sex addicts must learn that this is not true. . . . Stopping rituals is key to stopping sexual acting out. Rituals are all the thoughts and actions that lead to sexual acting out. —Mark Laaser[5]

What lust triggers do you continue to expose yourself to? How do you use sexual sin as a reward for completing a task or doing good? How much time do you spend looking at pornography each week? Do you have pornography hidden anywhere (physically or electronically)? Do you have any secret email accounts to receive sexual content?

- **Interacting with a real, anonymous person.** What website, phone numbers, or other services do you use to connect with these people? Have you put your name and contact information on any websites? Have you sent real pictures of yourself (nude or otherwise) or communicated through a webcam (casual or erotic)? Have you ever scheduled a time to meet someone? How many steps did you take toward meeting?

———

Questions after this point are for G4 participants who are married, engaged, or in a serious dating relationship where their sexual sin would be considered a betrayal of the commitment to exclusivity in that relationship. Such behaviors would be wrong even if you were not married, but as a Christ-follower who is married, your actions are also an offense against your spouse.

- **Emotional affair.** How did the relationship begin and when did the conversations become more trusting and self-disclosing? What negative statements have you made about your spouse, your marriage, or your family? What means of hidden communication do you have? When and where do you talk? What steps have you taken to hide this communication from your spouse? What has made it easier to hide this relationship? Have you jeopardized your employment with any of your actions?
- **Onetime sexual encounter.** How many people have you had "casual" sex with? When and how have you been the pursuer in these sexual encounters? When and how have you intentionally placed yourself in compromising situations so these encounters could occur? Has there been reason to fear pregnancy resulting from these sexual encounters? Have you paid for sex? Have you been tested for an STD?
- **Affair as a committed relationship.** Questions concerning an emotional affair are also relevant here. When did the sex begin? How did you meet and do you have frequent contact because of work or other shared settings? What expressions of love and commitment were exchanged (words, gifts, risks, trips, etc.)? Who knew about, condoned, or abetted the relationship?
- **Affair as a pseudo-spouse.** What plans have been made to leave your respective spouses? Who has met you and your adultery partner together? What actions have you taken to protect your adultery partner at the expense of your spouse and family? What lies have you told yourself or others about your spouse to validate your choices?

- **Illegal sexual sin.** If your sexual sin has crossed from only being immoral to also being illegal, your G4 group does not commit to keeping that information confidential. Sexual sin involving minors, filming or taking pictures of people without their consent, or coercive sexual activity will be reported to the appropriate legal authorities.

Accountability After Disclosure

This full disclosure exercise should not make your spouse your primary accountability partner. Doing so would place too great a weight on your spouse. Your spouse should not have the burden of either regularly asking you questions about your sexual sin or leaving you alone to battle your sin. However, that doesn't mean your spouse is barred from asking you about your sin and temptation. Not serving as your accountability partner frees them from the requirement of asking, but it does not prohibit them from asking. In addition, your spouse should be able to speak to your primary accountability partner(s) if they have concerns. Your spouse should also hear you confess if you succumb to temptation—which their primary accountability partner(s) will insist on.

> I hadn't asked her before bringing this sin into our home. If she was going to live with the consequences of it, then she had the right to determine what she needed to know. If we had any chance of rebuilding this marriage, there was no more room for lies or half-truths. In our groups, we answer more questions related to talking during adultery recovery than any other subject. We might have thought trust or forgiveness or even sex would come up most often, but, in reality, conversation is the bridge that can deliver trust, forgiveness, and sex.
> —Gary and Mona Shriver[6]

A WORD OF ENCOURAGEMENT

Completing a full disclosure is exhausting. But it is also important and pivotal work. At this point in the journey, many people are tempted to quit. They get to the precipice of freedom and then turn back because they realize freedom looks like honesty. Don't let that be you.

If you're scared or resistant to complete this step, be honest about it. Tell your group. They'll share their experience with Step 2, which undoubtedly involved fear and resistance. They'll also share with you how this step unlocked the door for significant change in their life because it allowed light into the darkest areas of their life. Don't pull back from this step until you've heard from others about the difference it made in their life.

G4 GROUP DISCUSSION: STEP 2, PART ONE

As you discuss this material in G4 group, these questions are meant to facilitate a more honest and beneficial dialogue about this material. Anyone is free to respond to whichever questions they choose.

> Completing a full disclosure is exhausting, but it is also pivotal.

Experienced Members

- How has the way you remember the development of your sexual sin changed during your time in G4?
- What was the most important insight you gleaned from tracing the history of your sexual sin?

New Members

- What part of tracing the history of your sexual sin was hardest for you to answer? Would you tell us a little about the internal obstacles you faced as you tried to be honest about it?
- What parts of your daily routine are most important to change?
- How can we pray for you?

Everyone

- What rituals or life rhythms, including nonsexual activities, are most important for you to change?
- How does the devotion on Proverbs 12 help you see the importance of completing a full disclosure?
- Have you experienced a significant setback or victory since last meeting that you should tell the group?

STEP 2
PART TWO

THE IMPACT OF YOUR SIN ON YOU

The video for this part of Step 2 can be found at: bradhambrick.com/falselove2p2.

Sin changes us. We cannot sin and remain the same. We want to believe that we can, but that is only one of the many lies we tell ourselves about our sin. Because we believe this lie we get upset with others who are affected by how we've changed. We say they are exaggerating, judgmental, or simply don't know what they're talking about. We tell ourselves those lies to reinforce the lie that sin hasn't changed us. Soon we have convinced ourselves that we are the only one who truly understands what is going on.

In this section you will be asked to evaluate ways that your sin has changed you. This begins with admitting that your sexual activity is morally wrong—that is, it is at odds with God's will for your life because it violates the first great commandment and it harms your relationship with those close to you because it violates the second great commandment. Sexual sin impairs our ability to love God with all our heart, soul, mind, and strength, and it interferes with our ability to love our neighbor as ourselves (Matthew 22:36–40).

Let's admit that as fallen people, all our sin feels "natural." This is why it's so easy for us to defend our sin. While we are committing our sin, it feels enjoyable, natural, and freeing. Our felt experience during moments of sin accounts for why we resist calling these actions sinful. And this is true for all sin. Lying feels necessary. Anger feels like righteous self-defense. Bitterness feels like remembering painful experiences. We cannot rely on our emotional reaction toward an activity to accurately determine whether that action is virtuous or sinful.

Remember, we are acknowledging the wrongness of our actions to help see and weigh our actions accurately. No one makes progress when their self-perception is distorted. The drunken person who believes they are only buzzed will not accurately assess their fitness to drive. When we minimize the impact of sexual sin on our relationship with God, self, and others, we will make comparably poor decisions.

We will use the following five-stage progression to explore the changes that sexual sin has on you: (1) image, (2) story, (3) risk, (4) sense of conquest, and (5) isolation. While no model captures every experience, this progression should build on your full disclosure work. It will allow you to see behind the behaviors of your sin and identify the way your sexual sin began to change you, your character, and your relationships.

> ▶ **Read James 1:12–15.** The Bible acknowledges that sin is especially tempting during stressful times of life (v. 12) and that temptation often follows a predictable progression (vv. 14–15). As you do this work in Step 2, we would join with James in warning you against blaming God for your temptation (v. 13). We often say things like "God made me with these desires" or "God brought this person into my life" as justification for our sin. James tells us that this is a misuse of the doctrine of God's providence. James also points out that temptation develops over time. Initially you feel lured by a desire for the act of sin and eventually you are drawn into the destructive effect of that sin (vv. 14–15). The progression below is meant to provide a way to trace that developmental process in the ways your sexual sin has shaped and changed you.

STAGE ONE: IMAGE

Sexual sin almost always begins with curiosity about the other gender. Pornography and romantic-themed media "teach" us about the opposite gender: what they look like, what they want, how they pursue romance, and how sex works. Temptation often initially feels like education. We feel ignorant, and temptation fills the void of our knowledge. The image stage may include the visual portrayal of the opposite gender's body or the portrayal of their character, skills, and persona.

You begin to see how an image changes from information to a standard—a criterion by which we measure members of the other gender and ourselves. We develop an appetite toward others that is born as we judge whether they measure up to our standard and preferences. Insecurity or pride emerges in ourselves based on whether we measure up to the ideal we're accepting. In stage one, we gain a type of knowledge that destroys freedom, peace, genuine care for others, and authenticity.

> ▶ **Read Genesis 2:15–3:24.** Adam had no images by which to measure himself or Eve so he was free to innocently delight in her (2:23). Satan tempted Eve with a kind of knowledge that promised freedom (3:4–5) but which ended in death and shame (3:6–7). Commonly referred to as "the fall," this moment changed the way that men and women relate to one another (3:16–19). Once the eyes of humanity were "opened" by sin, it would take the redemptive work of Jesus Christ for us to ever see rightly again. God graciously covered their shame (3:20) as a foreshadowing of Christ's death on the cross and took steps to limit the impact of the knowledge they had gained (3:22–24). But as innocent as stage one may seem, the cosmic changes between Genesis 2 and Genesis 3 sober us to the impact of this change.

For those whose lust is visually focused (often men), stage one gets entrenched as the "ideal image" and becomes the basis for discontentment in all real people. A set of physical traits and relational responses become an unrealistic expectation for their desire in a partner. Consider the following observation:

> How can a real woman—with pores and her own breasts and even sexual needs of her own . . . possibly compete with a cyber-vision of perfection, downloadable and extinguishable at will, who comes, so to speak, utterly submissive and tailored to the consumer's least specification? . . . Today, real naked women are just bad porn. —Naomi Wolf[1]

For those whose lust is narratively focused (often women), stage one gets entrenched as the "ideal romance" and becomes the basis for discontentment with real relationships. We will explore this more in stage two.

> ▶ **Reflection:** How has the "image" of an ideal romantic partner changed your relationship with self, others (especially current or future spouse), and God? How has a standard emerged that is hard for anyone, including yourself, to meet? How has that standard resulted in you doubting God's goodness to provide for you?

STAGE TWO: STORY

Neither men nor women find images exciting for long. Information needs a story to come alive. This is why we like movies—they're moving pictures with voices and a soundtrack. This is also why most media forms incorporate elements of story. Even benign clothing catalogs for winter apparel show their models doing something fun, like having a snowball fight, because it increases readers' response rate.

Pornography's biggest selling point is its story. Adultery is about more than finding a more attractive partner; it's about a new life without the stresses or problems of this one. We'll try to help you see that sexual sin is more narrative than it is visual. Understanding the role of story in sexual sin is important for understanding why God cares about our sexual lives. Masturbation is more than a socially awkward version of picking our nose; it is trying to escape into an alternative reality. We don't like the story God is writing for us and we want to write our own.

Men are aroused not merely by preferred body proportions. Men create a story wherein these well-proportioned women find them so attractive that they are drawn to them. It becomes a story of being powerful and revered. Pornography is a profitable industry that tells these stories of women who find a man irresistible. In pornography, professional storytellers and professional actors set fantasies to a soundtrack. Men like getting lost in the idea that "this could be me."

Romantic-themed media, which is often more appealing to women, has a similar approach. There is a story of ideal romance. In a stereotypical romantic comedy, the lead female character is the sole object of the lead male character's attention. He does all he can to win her favor. She is the center of the universe in this story. Comparably, in movies portraying forbidden love, the entire narrative is about their struggle to be together and the ecstatic joy they find when they finally belong to one another. Risk, struggle, adoration, disappointment, and waiting are all woven into the suspense that ends happily ever after.

The result is that "story" and "reality" can never match. No marriage comes with a soundtrack. Noticeably absent from pornography or romantic-themed media is everyday life. There is no mundane—only variety and excitement. There is no waiting or disappointment, only foreshadowing. The characters do not have to make difficult decisions together with limited resources of time and money when their personal goals conflict. Nobody ever gets tired. Who wouldn't want to live in that world? The following testimony gives this view:

> Because, see, if I'm going to have sex with my wife, I'll have to put down the novel, brush my teeth, and find out how she's really doing. And I guess we should use birth control, just in case. Then I'll have to ask what she's thinking about, how her day has gone, whether she bought the new dress after work, and things like that. I'll have to tell her a few things about my day, too, even though I'd rather not think about most of it. I'll have to hold her, caress her, let her know she's important, and undertake an act that I may not be able to consummate. Or, I'll be left feeling that I didn't care enough about her sexual needs. No, I think I'll stick with the marching words on the next page and masturbate. —Harry Schaumburg[2]

It can be easy for those who are caught in the sin of adultery to look down on the fiction world of pornography because of pornography's fantasy basis. But adultery is every bit as much fantasy as pornography. Adultery may be a relationship with a real person, but it is not a "real relationship."

You put far more time, energy, planning, and preparation into adultery sex than you ever would marital sex—the deceptive nature of adultery demands it. You get to be "on" every time you see one another. You fight together against villains, which include your spouses and whatever else prevents you from being together. The fact that your interactions must be secret adds an element of delightful suspense that would evaporate when or if the relationship were no longer forbidden. You cannot criticize one another at this stage because you are sinning "for" one another rather than "against" one another.

> ▶ **Reflection:** How has the "story" of an ideal romance or romance partner changed your relationship with self, others (especially current or future spouse), and God? How have you lost the ability to be content with normal life events and relationships? How have you begun to resent God for things you believe he is withholding from you?

> Adultery is every bit as much fantasy as pornography.

STAGE THREE: RISK

Sexual sin is not willing to merely look at an image or watch a story. It wants to be part of the story. Eventually that involves taking risks to make it happen. A primary expression of sexuality is excitement. Indeed, we call sexuality's effect on the body *arousal*. This helps to explain why risk, especially in sinful or destructive sexual experiences, is used to increase the pleasure gained.

Risk is a significant factor in why sexual sin inevitably grows. Once something has been experienced several times, it becomes common. As the risk factor is reduced, the enjoyment of that experience seems less intense. At first, you are afraid of getting caught and this adds to the risk of any action you take. As you become more comfortable with the action, you are willing to take more risks. The following quotes express that risk—a misplaced excitement:

Danger and excitement are kissing cousins in affairs. —Harry Schaumburg[3]

Sex addicts sexualize most situations and see some sexual humor in it. Sexual jokes can be used to recruit new sexual partners. Sex addicts can gauge the reaction of a person hearing their sexual joke, and if that reaction is favorable, the level of sexual engagement might be taken one step higher. —Mark Laaser[4]

This higher and higher level of risk often results in the exposure of sexual sin. Sexuality feeds on risk. In a healthy marriage, risk goes by the name *vulnerability* as a couple knows and celebrates each other at deeper and deeper levels. However, in sexual sin, risk grows in destructive ways because it does not have a wholesome expression. Instead, it shows up in more perverse themes of pornography, more overt fishing for sexual partners in social settings, or more open communication with one's adultery partner.

> ▶ **Reflection:** How has the risk stage of lust changed your relationship with self, others (especially current or future spouse), and God? What actions do you now take without fear that once scared you? What risks are you currently taking? If those risks become common during the next year, what new risks would you be willing to take?

STAGE FOUR: SENSE OF CONQUEST

Sex is not only powerful because it is intense, but it is about power because it creates change. **Read 1 Corinthians 6:15–7:4.** When we have sex with someone, we unite with them (6:16) and we belong to each other (7:4). This is why the expression of lust from one person to another is "I want to *have* them." This is why people believe that they will feel more confident or secure if they can have sex with someone they esteem as beautiful or important. When we use sex to try to change things about ourselves or our lives that we don't like, we are using sex for its power.

However, the notion that sex can be tamed this way—that it can be used to make me feel more confident or secure—is a lie. Sex outside of God's design can no more be tamed than a lightning bolt outside an electrical system. Sex used for power is sex being used like a drug. We look for a more powerful experience because the previous experience didn't "work" (i.e., have the lasting effect we desired). In *Closing the Window: Steps to Living Porn Free*, the author writes,

> Instead of the image of the pressure cooker needing periodic release, the Bible speaks of sin as slavery, entanglement, and captivity. Sin crouches at our door waiting to control us (Genesis 4:7). The more we indulge our sinful desires, the

stronger they become. When we give in to temptation, the temptation goes away, but only for a short time. Lust comes back, sooner and stronger than it did before. —Tim Chester[5]

We begin to see that the conquest stage of sexual sin explains why our appetite grows. Climbing a mountain doesn't make you content to live on the prairie. Instead, it creates an appetite to climb a taller mountain. With a conquest mindset, we are fundamentally using sex for the wrong purpose. God made sex to be a source of joy through serving someone we voluntarily belong to, not a way for us to demand satisfaction by those we want to belong to us.

> ▶ **Reflection:** How has the conquer stage of lust changed your relationship with self, others (especially current or future spouse), and God? How has the conquer stage changed your role in sex from servant of someone you love to owner or judge? How has the conquer stage changed your view of sex from the celebration of a committed relationship to an expression of recreation from which you expect optimal pleasure and benefit?

STAGE FIVE: ISOLATION

Sexual sin is like drinking salt water. When you are thirsty, salt water looks satisfying. But when you drink salt water, you only get thirstier. When you are lonely, bored, stressed, or angry, sexual sin looks like companionship, entertainment, relief, or revenge (more on this in Step 3). But when you partake in sexual sin, you only become lonelier, more bored with real life, more stressed, and more angry or defensive.

> Trying to cure distress with the same thing that caused it is typically the mechanism that closes the trap on an addict. —Cornelius Plantinga Jr.[6]

Trying to cure loneliness with sexual sin is like trying to put out a fire with gasoline. Sometimes it makes sense to put out a fire with liquid, but gasoline is a flammable liquid. In the same way, sexual sin exacerbates loneliness. As we sin, we distance ourselves from God and authentic relationships. Until we take a definitive step to openly confess our sin and forsake it, we will continue to drink the salt water of sexual sin. We'll experience short-term relief and long-term anguish.

▶ **Reflection:** How has the isolation of lust changed your relationship with self, others (especially current or future spouse), and God? What thirsts (i.e., legitimate longings) are you trying to quench when you engage in sexual sin? How has your sexual sin actually made these thirsts more intense?

SUMMARIZE HOW YOU'VE CHANGED

Look back over your reflections for each of the five stages of progression in sexual sin—(1) image, (2) story, (3) risk, (4) sense of conquest, and (5) isolation. Think back to your initial reaction to the statement "Sin changes us. We cannot sin and remain the same." What was your initial reaction to that statement? How much did you expect to discover that sin has changed you? Chances are it was far less than your actual discovery. If so, don't let that be a point of shame. The fact that you can acknowledge how much your sin has changed you is a sign that God's grace is active in your life.

Apart from God's grace, we would strongly resist owning up to these changes. Sometimes God's grace is unpleasant, especially when God is removing something wedged deep in our soul that doesn't belong there. But you are now cooperating with God's grace. That's a good thing. Be encouraged.

G4 GROUP DISCUSSION: STEP 2, PART TWO

As you discuss this material in G4 group, these questions are meant to facilitate a more honest and beneficial dialogue about this material. Anyone is free to respond to whichever questions they choose.

Experienced Members

- Reflecting on the Tim Chester quote, how did giving into sexual sin make your urges stronger instead of giving you relief (as we often tell ourselves it will)?
- Have you come to see that the statement "adultery is every bit as much fantasy as pornography" is true?

New Members

- From the James 1 devotional, how have you been prone to blame God for your struggle?

- What risks are you currently taking in pursuit of your sexual sin that you never thought you would take?
- How can we pray for you?

Everyone

- In what ways can you relate to the salt water analogy?
- From the Genesis 2–3 devotional, what loss of innocence have you experienced due to lust? How can you begin to see that innocence is actually good and not a negative synonym for "juvenile"?
- Have you experienced a significant setback or victory since last meeting that you should tell the group?

> The fact that you can acknowledge how much your sin has changed you is a sign God's grace is active in your life.

STEP 2
PART THREE

THE IMPACT OF YOUR SIN ON OTHERS

The video for this part of Step 2 can be found at: bradhambrick.com/falselove2p3.

S in is not tame. It will not stay on command like a domesticated puppy. Sin refuses to remain within the limited areas of our life that we think we can allot for sin. Sin is wild. It is a predator (1 Peter 5:8). And once we unleash sin in our life, we cannot manage the damage it does. Pretending that we, in our own strength, are stronger than our sin is another lie we've believed for a long time.

Many of us wish our sin would only impact *us*. It is as if we try to make a deal with Satan: "Ravage my life if you want. I'm the one doing the bad thing. But leave my loved ones alone. Don't mess with them because of what I'm doing." Sin refuses the deal. It would be like playing with matches and then begging the fire to only burn down your room in the house. That is not how fire operates, and it is not how sin works.

For this reason, whether you meant for it to or not, your sin has affected many people in your life. Step 2 acknowledges the breadth and impact of your sin, examining how your sin has impacted others. This is part of change. Sin is self-focused. It focuses on *my* pleasure, *my* relief, and *my* preferences to the neglect of others. Repentance is the foundation of change, and it requires that we begin to be focused on others.

In this part of Step 2, you will examine four groups of people who could be affected by your sexual sin: (1) your spouse and children (if married), (2) friends with whom you have been less than authentic, (3) the opposite gender for whom you have warped expectations, and (4) your adultery partner and his/her family (in the case of extramarital sex).

56

THE IMPACT ON YOUR SPOUSE AND CHILDREN

Part of the change process is being emotionally sturdy enough to face the consequences of our sin. Talking about the impact of your sin on your spouse and children may generate shame or defensiveness. That is understandable, but it can no longer be a reason to avoid the question. They didn't get to choose the pain your sin introduced into their life. You shouldn't give yourself the option not to acknowledge the impact of your sin in their life.

It would be selfish and wrong to just say that you know what you did was wrong and claim everyone should move on. That would force your family to carry alone the pain you've generated in their life. Someone genuinely desiring to change and demonstrate they are trustworthy would not do that.

The most important thing that you can do for your spouse at this stage is to provide an honest, full disclosure. The most damaging thing you could do is a partial disclosure that you claim is a full disclosure. So many marriages at this stage die the death of a thousand confessions—that is, partial disclosures where more is acknowledged as more is discovered. One woman gave the following testimony to her counselor, Stefanie Carnes:

> There were several major disclosures over six months. I was completely devastated. He continued to disclose half-truths, only increasing my pain and making the situation worse. Each new disclosure was like reliving the initial pain all over again. I wish the truth had been disclosed all at once and not in bits and pieces. —Stefanie Carnes[1]

Conversation with spouse: After your full disclosure, you should ask your spouse "How has my sexual sin impacted you?" If your spouse is going through the accompanying *True Betrayal* study, they will be assessing that in Step 3 of their journey. Be patient until your spouse gets to that point. When they share something, own the impact of your sin, apologize for the impact, and thank them for giving you important information for your growth.

Conversation with children: After conversation with your spouse, you should be willing to engage the question "How is my sin impacting our children?" If direct conversations with your children are wise and needed, do not put your spouse in the position of having these conversations alone. Appendix B walks you and your spouse through the process of determining when and how to talk with your children, based on the appropriateness of their age and changes being made to the family dynamics. The most important thing that you can do is to actively engage the process of change. You cannot protect your children from past sin, but you can protect them from present sin, passivity, and cowardice.

THE IMPACT ON YOUR FRIENDS

You will be asked to create a chart to help you complete this section (see sample below). In column one, list the secrets you've withheld or the lies you've told about your sexual sin. Don't cop out by saying there are "too many to remember." The longer you wait to be honest, the longer the list of lies. Review your notes from Part Three of Step 1, "Both Lust and Lying," as you compile this list.

> You cannot protect your loved ones from past sin, but you can protect them from present sin, passivity, and cowardice.

In column two, list the people impacted by each secret or lie. You might list multiple names in column two for each secret or lie. This column will require reflection. Once you get in the habit of living deceptively, you can easily become mindless about your lies. Completing this column requires giving thought to those who are still living under the false pretense of your past lies.

In column three, describe how the absence of accurate information (i.e., secrets withheld) or the presence of false information (i.e., lies told) negatively impacted each relationship. In some instances, you may know concrete ways the other person was impacted. In other instances, you may not be as sure. When you get to Step 5 and begin to make amends with these people, it is appropriate to ask, "Are there ways my sin and deceit impacted you that I am unaware of?"

> ▶ **Read Hebrews 3:12–14.** You might be tempted to think that making this chart is a way of taking your punishment. That is not true. This exercise is not punitive; it is liberating. Transparency

is one of the primary ways that God intends to protect us from sin. Whether it feels comfortable to you now or not, you want people to know you. Until you are willing to be known by the people who love you, the fictional story of sexual sin will be too strong for you to resist alone. Allowing people to know you daily combats being "hardened by the deceitfulness of sin" (v. 13).

SECRETS / LIES	RELEVANT PEOPLE WHO DON'T KNOW	IMPACT ON RELATIONSHIP
Having a secret credit card for expenses related to pornographic websites.	Spouse	Spouse: False understanding of family finances and rationale for financial sacrifices.
	Small Group Friends	Small Group: False sense that I was being more honest than I was.
Using lunch break to date adultery partner who is your direct report at work.	Spouse	Spouse: Your work now threatens the marriage instead of supporting the marriage.
	Boss	Boss: You are violating company policies and creating a work environment that will be problematic as your sin inevitably becomes public.
	Church Friend at Work	Church Friend: Feels gullible for trusting you, questions whether they inadvertently covered for you, or wonders if they falsely vouched for your character at church.

In Step 5, we will recommend that you begin the process of making things right with these people. At this stage in your journey, you are disavowing yourself of the notion that your sexual sin didn't impact anyone else. You are learning to be empathetic toward the impact of your sin on others so that when you confess, your efforts at making things right in those relationships will be more effective.

THE IMPACT ON OUR VIEW OF THE OTHER GENDER

Sin turns differences that should be honored into qualities that are judged. If we deem those qualities desirable, we call that judgment lust; and if we deem those qualities undesirable, the judgment is expressed as condemnation. Our culture strongly ranks people based on appearance, and because culture is merely the coalescence of thousands of individuals' choices, our sinful choices contribute to the cultural corrosion. Our sin adds to the cultural decay, rather than providing the salt and light influence that God intended (Matthew 5:13–16).

One unnoticed impact of sexual sin is the way it magnifies the natural differences in gender. The more men or women engage in pornography, the more professional storytellers make a normal man or woman in a normal relationship seem "less than." The more men or women engage in adultery, the more a lover on their best behavior who is only engaged in moments of forbidden love makes marriage with its weight of normal life choices seem unfulfilling and dull.

> ▶ **Question:** How have your expectations of the other gender changed? How has your sexual sin changed the way you define "a good man" or "a good woman" or "a good marriage"? What gender stereotypes have become more deeply ingrained in how you think because of your sexual sin?

THE IMPACT ON YOUR ADULTERY PARTNER AND FAMILY

Consideration for an adultery partner should be at the bottom of your priority list, but it is often the top concern for people coming out of an adulterous relationship. Pause and realize that if your adultery partner was married, you should have greater remorse toward their spouse and children than toward your adultery partner. They are the ones unknowingly hurt by your actions. If that is not what your emotions are saying, realize this reveals a lack of emotional clarity.

While it may be hard to hear, the greatest blessing you can give your adultery partner is to remove the temptation for further sexual sin. That means cutting off all contact. If you are wondering, there is simply *no* easy way to end a relationship that should have never started.

The natural rebuttal is "But I really care about this person and don't want to hurt them." The reality is that when a sinful relationship gets started, someone is going to get hurt and usually multiple people. Think about it. How are you going to get out of the situation you're in without hurting someone? You can't. You will not make wise decisions if you are holding out hope that an impossible reality is possible. The following things are true at this moment:

- You will hurt one or more people that you care about.
- You will have to be more honest with more people than you want to be.
- You won't find an easy answer that makes this situation just go away.
- Your life will radically change based upon what you do with what you're reading.
- Your family will be affected for generations based on what you do.

Even if you choose to ignore these things now, you will have to acknowledge them as reality at some point, and the longer you wait the more intense the consequences will be for everyone involved. With that in mind, consider these actions:

1. **Cut off all contact.** Clearly state that you are requesting no future contact for any reason. Document this request. If your adultery partner continues to pursue you and stalking behaviors emerge, a restraining order may be needed. The main point is to clearly request no future contact.

2. **Disclose all forms of contact.** Any means of contact should be disclosed to your spouse (e.g., secret cell phone, secret email address, rendezvous times in your schedule, etc.). When you end the relationship, you should tell your adultery partner that all these forms of contact have been disclosed to your spouse.

   Also, disclose all *attempted* contact. Ending an adulterous relationship requires more than doing the right thing one time. If your adultery occurred in an ongoing relationship, the other person will likely not want the relationship to end. Your adultery partner will likely fight for the relationship they thought they had.

   It is vital that you disclose any contact or attempted contact by your adultery partner to your spouse. Even if you get a phone call from an unknown number, choose not to answer it. If they leave no voicemail, tell your spouse. If a friend of the adultery partner gives you a note, refuse to read it and tell your spouse.

   You may think this sounds harsh. It is not mean; it is definitive. It is choosing to honor your marriage and relinquish your sin. This doesn't mean you won't grieve. It does mean there is a clear path for honoring God in this situation.

3. **Open communication.** "Open" should mean that your spouse or someone your spouse trusts to represent them is copied on any email or present for any meeting. One way we reveal who we love most is by who we talk to about another. That means when you talked about your spouse to your adultery partner, it revealed that your primary allegiance was to your adultery partner. Now, you are reversing this allegiance by insisting that your spouse is aware of all communication.

4. **Avoid the "Closure Trap."** There is no such thing as closure after adultery. *Closure* is a word that gives the impression of a settled, happy ending. One of the two romantic relationships in your life will die an awkward, painful death. More uncomfortable still, you are going to decide which relationship ends (your marriage or your adultery relationship).

   You might ask, "Why are you being so graphic and harsh?" The reason is simple: "Closure" is the lie most people believe that leads them back into adultery multiple times even while they claim they are trying to restore their marriage. Closure is an innocent word that masks its devastating consequences.

CONCLUSION

Step 2 stings. It required us to examine things we would rather ignore. It removed the emotional buffer of minimizing our sin. That is both hard and good. If you are tired or your motivation to finish this journey is waning, acknowledge that to your G4 group, counselor, or accountability partner. This step is hard. There is no shame in being tired.

At the same time, do not lose sign of the fact that this step is good. There is no path to peace that doesn't traverse through honesty. The less honest you've been in recent months and years, the more Step 2 will sting. That sting is like pouring peroxide on an infected wound. The bubbling reaction and sting indicate that something good is happening. Allow the testimonies of more experienced G4 group members to encourage you as you hear the importance of this step in their journey.

G4 GROUP DISCUSSION: STEP 2, PART THREE

As you discuss this material in G4 group, these questions are meant to facilitate a more honest and beneficial dialogue about this material. Anyone is free to respond to whichever questions they choose.

Experienced Members

- Looking back, how did Step 2 play a vital role in your journey?
- What were the most tangible ways that Part Three of Step 2 made you more other-focused?

New Members

- If you are married, are you committed to be fully honest with your spouse?
- Where or how do you most need to grow in courage to complete Step 2?
- How can we pray for you?

> There is no path to peace that doesn't traverse through honesty.

Everyone

- Who have you lied to or hid from, and how has it impacted them?
- From the devotional in Hebrews 3, do you view the work of Step 2 as taking your punishment or guidance toward freedom?
- Have you experienced a significant setback or victory since last meeting that you should tell the group?

STEP 3
UNDERSTAND the origin, motive, and history of my sin.

At the end of this step, I want to be able to say . . .

**"I do not know all I need to know about myself
or my sin. I do know my heart resists being known
(Jeremiah 17:9), and that my cravings reveal the
things that are most important to me (Luke 6:45).
I am coming to realize that [list specific desires]
lead me to sin, and that [list key past experiences]
have contributed to the strength of those desires.
However, I believe God is more satisfying
than those desires could ever be without him
and that a life honoring him can reshape
the strength of my desires."**

STEP 3

PART ONE

LEARNING LESSONS FROM MY HISTORY OF SIN

The video for this part of Step 3 can be found at: bradhambrick.com/falselove3p1.

We often fall into the trap of thinking that if we understand the "why" better, then the "what" will be easy—or at least easier. At least two realities should subvert this seemingly sound logic.

First, sin is not rational, so it refuses to play by our rules of logic. Sin is not a simple behavior that operates according to single-variable motivations. Rather sin is a condition and a predator. Sin has its roots in our fallen human nature. Sin is aided and abetted by an enemy who desires our destruction (1 Peter 5:8). This means that sin both has the home-field advantage and is willing to cheat to win.

Second, our goal must be effectiveness at change rather than ease of change. Sin is always willing to wait for a more opportune time (Luke 4:13). Our intelligent adversary will strike during the moments when we let our guard down. Therefore, anything that decreases our vigilance is an asset to our adversary.

These realities do not make an examination of the history and motives of our sin fruitless, but it means that what we intuitively want from this examination is often overly optimistic. We will glean important information that allows us to be more intentional and strategic on our journey, but our journey will not be easier because of that knowledge. Rather, it will make us more effective on what will remain a difficult journey. With that in mind, we will divide the work of Step 3 into three parts: learning lessons from my history of sin; identifying the motives for my sin; and capturing my present struggle.

CHRONICLING MY HISTORY OF SEXUAL SIN

As you do the work of chronicling your history of sexual sin, your goal is to gather information that helps you ask better questions. Asking better questions will allow you to gain a better understanding of your struggle. Understanding your struggle better will help you fight your sin more strategically, and having a more strategic plan should allow you to be more effective.

That previous paragraph sounds crisp, logical, and sequential. However, the work of Step 3 may not feel that way, especially at first. The early work of Step 3 may feel like putting dots on a piece of paper. Each dot represents a meaningful piece of information about your history. Which dots are most significant or what picture best emerges from the dots may not be immediately obvious. Initially, you may only be able to say, "I have more dots than I had before."

> Anything that decreases our vigilance is an asset to our adversary.

Over time, your actions will begin to feel like less of a mystery to you. As you do the history work of Step 3, in Part One you will focus on your past. In Step 3, Parts Two and Three, you'll shift your focus to the present. As a whole, Step 3 will allow you to gain the advantages described in the opening paragraph of this section.

To be clear, understanding our sinful tendencies better does not justify our sin, but it is helpful in overcoming our sin. It is like the "aha moment" when someone realizes that their frequent upset stomach is related to lactose intolerance, or their constant fatigue is correlated with sleep apnea. Understanding doesn't remove the problem, but it makes the needed changes more obvious.

▶ **Read Exodus 2:11–12.** Moses's sin struggle was anger rather than lust. But Moses gives us an example of the type of work we're doing in this part of Step 3. Moses's anger was not random. Moses's history helps his sin make sense without excusing his actions. Moses was Jewish. The Egyptians had murdered all the Jewish boys his age. His people were still slaves in Egypt while Moses, through a series of providential events, grew up in Pharaoh's household. When he sees an Egyptian beating a Jewish man (v. 11), he is furious and murders the Egyptian (v. 12). If Moses was going to rein in his anger, he would need to deal with his history in a healthier manner. In a similar way, we are studying our history to determine how it might contribute to our sin.

To chronicle the history of your sexual sin, we'll explore seven areas, arranged chronologically throughout your life. We'll describe the impact and relevance of each and then provide you with reflection questions to help you write your own story.

1. **How did you learn about sex?** How we learn about something has a large impact on what you do with it. A mean kindergarten teacher shapes how a student thinks about school. An embarrassing gotcha question from a middle-school friend about sex can result in feeling intimidated by sexuality. The first thing we know about a subject and how we learned it has a large impact on how we think about it. The tone of the learning experience is also powerful. It teaches you whether a subject is safe, good, clean, dirty, casual, secretive, or sacred.
   - How did you learn about sex?
   - Who initially taught you about sex?
   - Was it wholesome, accurate, and age-appropriate or dirty, inaccurate, and premature?
   - Were you allowed to ask questions, or did you have to learn through curiosity and exploration?

2. **What were your first sexual experiences?** First experiences make an impression. They set the tone for an experience and become the basis for expectations. For instance, the first time you said "I love you," to someone you were dating and their response will have a big impact on the type of relational risks you are willing to take in the future (i.e., being vulnerable). First experiences are the normal we know until something significant changes our perspective on that event or activity.
   - When do you first remember being attracted to someone?
   - When was your first dating relationship, and how did it go?
   - When did you begin to experiment with masturbation, and how was the practice introduced to you?

- What were your first sexual experiences with holding hands, kissing, petting, and intercourse?
- Were you ever touched inappropriately as a child?
- Were you exposed to sexual material (pornography) or sexual activity (abuse) as a child or young person?

3. **What was your family history related to sex and affection?** Family is where we develop our sense of belonging. In the family, we gain a baseline expectation for whether love is available, must be earned, or is dangerous. Patterns and styles of affection are first experienced in our families of origin. For instance, some families are highly profuse in their words of encouragement toward one another; others are not. Some families hug a lot; others rarely touch. Your preferred style of affection learned in your family of origin can impact how you engage with social and romantic relationships.

- Were your parents affectionate to one another and the children?
- Were compliments freely given in your home?
- How often did your family talk about their day and express interest in each other's lives?
- What family rules or patterns made authenticity and vulnerability more or less appealing?
- What was your family's style of discipline: power, guilt, positive modeling of appropriate behaviors, permissiveness, etc.?
- Did your parents talk about sex comfortably, crudely, shamefully, or not at all?
- Were you aware of any infidelity between your parents or sexual sin by your parents?

4. **What is your personal style of relating?** No personality or temperament is immune from the struggle with sexual sin. But the values expressed by our personality and temperament influence which sins we are more prone toward and the form those sins take. For example, an extrovert might like the variety of pornography while an introvert is more attracted to its anonymity.

- Does being with people energize you or drain you?
- Do you prefer fiction over reality?

- Do you prefer to pursue or be pursued in a relationship?
- How do you handle emotions like guilt, shame, and disappointment?
- How comfortable do you feel expressing emotions or putting yourself into words?
- How many meaningful same-sex friendships do you have?
- To whom do you confide your fears, struggles, and temptations?

5. **How do you use your time and manage stress?** Sexual sin requires time. More specifically, it requires time away from people, especially people who would be a good influence in your life. Also, escaping stress is one of the most common reasons for engaging in sexual sin. For these reasons, your schedule and use of time matter.
   - To whom are you accountable for how you use your time (friend, spouse, boss, etc.)?
   - Do your current personal commitments fit within a 168-hour week (seven 24-hour days)? Are you trying to do more than can be done with the time God has provided? Do your expectations of yourself exceed God's expectations for you?
   - Have you examined your schedule to ensure that your priorities have first dibs on your schedule?
   - How much sleep do you get each night? Are you honoring the fact that God made you a finite human being and graciously called you to rest, or are you trying to be superhuman?

6. **What is your ongoing sexual history?** Your ongoing sexual history should be a continuation of the full disclosure you began in Step 2. If you are acting out, your full disclosure should be an active document—meaning that you should be updating it as God and this study brings more to mind. You want to update this document for two reasons: First, it is a means of practicing continued honesty with God, self, and others. Second, it may also be used in honesty with your spouse as you strive to show yourself to be a person of integrity.

7. **What meaning do you give to sex?** Here we begin to see how history bleeds into motive (Step 3, Part Two). We ultimately attach

meaning to sex based on our own history: Sex is power, sex is love, sex is free, sex is meaningless, sex is a weapon, sex is leverage, etc. We can attribute more than one meaning to sex. The meaning we give to sex may be accurate or inaccurate; it may contribute to our holiness or our depravity. But, to change the meaning we give to sex, we need to be able to articulate it.

- Before doing the work of Step 3, Part Two, give your first impression to the following questions: What meaning do you give to sex? What life struggles or unpleasant emotions do you use sex to assuage?

CONCLUSION

You probably remember a history teacher repeating a version of the adage "Those who don't study history are doomed to repeat it." As it applies to our subject, we might say, "A mindless life is a directionless life that repeats destructive patterns." If we don't ask important questions, we'll repeat existing behaviors. That is why we are doing this work. We realize it's a problem if we continue sinning.

As you complete this part of Step 3, you may not have an amazing insight that gives significant direction to how you're seeking to change. That's okay. If you did gain insight, that's wonderful. Either way, your future work on this journey will be richer for having done the hard work of this reflection. Even if the benefit only emerges in small insights along the way, it has been a worthwhile investment.

G4 GROUP DISCUSSION: STEP 3, PART ONE

As you discuss this material in G4 group, these questions are meant to facilitate a more honest and beneficial dialogue about this material. Anyone is free to respond to whichever questions they choose.

Experienced Members

- What benefits did you gain from this part of Step 3 that were not immediately obvious to you?
- How have discussions around this part of Step 3 allowed you to be more supportive of fellow G4 members?

New Members

- Were you encouraged or disappointed by the initial insight developed from this part of Step 3?
- Are there prompt changes you need to make in the way you manage time and stress?
- How can we pray for you?

Everyone

- Recall Moses's anger and his resulting sin in the Exodus 2 devotional. What insights from your history have you been able to identify that contribute to your struggle toward sexual integrity?

> A mindless life is a directionless life that repeats destructive patterns.

- Based on your style of relating, are there ways that this group can be more effective at supporting you in your G4 journey?
- Have you experienced a significant setback or victory since last meeting that you should tell the group?

STEP 3
PART TWO

IDENTIFYING THE MOTIVES FOR MY SIN

The video for this part of Step 3 can be found at: bradhambrick.com/falselove3p2.

N ow we turn to identifying the motives behind our sin. Our goal in the second part of Step 3 is twofold: (a) to put our motives into clear words, and (b) to find better words for responding to our motives. Naming our motives allows others to know us better and, thereby, support us more effectively. Talking about our motives helps us circumvent white-knuckle change.

We will look at fifteen motives that are frequently associated with sexual sin. This list is not meant to be exhaustive, but it represents many of the gains we try to derive from our sinful behaviors. If you don't find your motive on the list, then reading through the list should allow you to put into words what you're trying to get from your sin.

TRIGGERS AND MOTIVES

Often triggers and motive are treated as two distinct things, and there are differences. But those differences are more akin to two sides of the same coin rather than two distinct items like apples and oranges. The things that trigger (i.e., prompt) us to sin usually reveal what we want from our sin (i.e., motives). For that reason, as we list a trigger, we'll also list the probable motive associated with that prompt toward sin.

As you work through this material, you are encouraged to ask yourself these two questions:

- Which of these prompts fit me best?
- What does the corresponding motive reveal about how I'm using my sin?

Your answer to the second question will serve as a significant bridge between Step 3 and Step 4. Let's explore each of fifteen potential motives for your sin.

1. **Boredom (sin as my joy).** When boredom is our trigger, then sin has become our joy. In a dull moment when we could choose what to pursue, we choose sin rather than God or any of his legitimate pleasures. By doing this, we begin to lose our appetite for godly pleasure—like the child who eats sweets before dinner and then finds vegetables unappealing. Even as the child feels sluggish from the ups and downs of sugary treats, they fail to connect this to their diet but go instead for another sugar high as the obvious solution. In the book *Sexual Detox: A Guide for Guys Who Are Sick of Porn*, we read the following:

   > Sex is not ultimate. . . . Idols begin as good things to which we give too much importance, and few things slide over into idolatry with greater frequency or greater power than sex. We allow a good gift of God to supersede the God who gave it. Sex is good, even great, but it's not ultimate. —Tim Challies[1]

   ▶ **Read Nehemiah 8:9–12.** God is a God of joy and pleasure. Too often we view God as so serious that we believe fun must be in the opposite direction from God. When God called Israel to repentance, he asked them to express their repentance in celebration. If the motive of boredom leads you to sin, then allow this passage to challenge your view of God.

2. **Loneliness (sin as my friend).** When loneliness is our trigger, it reveals we're treating sin like our friend. Sexual sin is always relational whether the relationship is fictional (pornography) or physical (adultery), so it answers loneliness well. It is as if our sin calls to us to confide our troubles. We are glad to pull up a chair and unload. As we accept this counterfeit relief, talking to a real person begins to feel too risky. We now fear being judged or known by anyone but our faux friend sin.

▶ **Read Proverbs 27:6.** During sexual sin we write this proverb backwards. We believe, "Faithful are the kisses of an enemy; profuse are the wounds of a friend." When sin reverses the roles of friend and enemy, it has trapped us. If the motive of loneliness leads you to sexual sin, then prayerfully examine who or what you are calling "friend."

3. **Stress (sin as my comforter).** When stress is our trigger, sin has become our comforter. We run to it, her, or him. And for a short time, sin seems to make things better. The comfort, however, takes on an addictive quality. The stress that we're seeking relief from is actually multiplied by the stress our sin creates. This keeps us in a cycle of stress and returning to a primary source of stress for relief.

    ▶ **Read John 14:25–31.** In verse 26, Jesus describes the Holy Spirit as "the Helper" (ESV) or "the Comforter" (KJV) and as the source of peace that is distinct from the world's peace (v. 27). If a source of comfort does not allow you to be more authentic with the people who care about you, then it does not give true comfort. Instead, it is a drug that numbs you before it makes you sick. If the motive of stress leads you to sexual sin, then examine whether your comfort is real or a form of self-medication.

4. **Frustration (sin as my peace).** When frustration is our trigger, then sin has become our source of peace. Sin is treated like an oasis. When this happens, we label sin as our safe place. After we do this, we villainize anyone or anything that opposes or interferes with our sin. For this reason, we begin to distance ourselves from those who care about us.

    ▶ **Read Romans 16:17–20 and 1 Thessalonians 5:22–24.** Notice that each of the passages refer to knowing the God of peace as the alternative to falling into temptations. Where you turn for peace reveals whether you are growing in godliness or worldliness. Once you declare something your source of peace, you will be fiercely loyal and obedient to it.

5. **Fatigue (sin as my source of life).** When fatigue is our trigger, sin has become our source of life. We turn to sin for a boost to get through the day. We begin to use the energy "boost" from viewing pornography or a flirtatious conversation like we would coffee. The thought of our sin keeps us going when we feel like giving up.

    ▶ **Read 2 Corinthians 4:7–18.** This passage uses many words that can be associated with fatigue: *afflicted* (v. 8), *perplexed* (v. 8), *persecuted* (v. 9), *struck down* (v. 9), and *wasting away* (v. 16). Paul reminds us to turn to Christ to counter the fatiguing effect of living in a fallen world (vv. 10–12). Otherwise, the things we turn to for a boost become weights that further exhaust us.

6. **Hurt (sin as my refuge).** When hurt is our trigger, sin has become our refuge. In our moments of sinful escape, we feel protected by our sin. As a result, a growing allegiance develops between us and our sin. In reality, our sexual sin provides as much protection as covers pulled over a child's head, but in our moment of hurt we are appreciative for even the facade of refuge we think our sin provides.

    ▶ **Read Psalm 31.** This psalm alternates between a cry for help and a song of confidence. Psalm 31 is an example of the realness with which Scripture speaks to life. Sexual sin is a pseudo-refuge on demand. Even when we cannot have the sin, we can fantasize about a lover's presence. We turn to lust as a mental escape. However, the real refuge in God is available through prayerful meditation as modeled in Psalm 31. Prayer is more than a fantasy; it is conversation with the real God who promises his presence and involvement in our hardships.

7. **Betrayal (sin as my revenge).** When betrayal is our trigger, sin has become our revenge. We know how powerful betrayal is (especially sexual betrayal), so we decide to use its power to get revenge against those who have hurt us. Blinded by pain, we try to create pain to get even. We are blinded to the reality that we are only multiplying pain. This approach never offers anyone less pain.

▶ **Read Romans 12:17–21.** It is so tempting to read this passage as God withholding sweet relief and satisfaction from you. Instead, it is God withholding even more pain from you. God is not removing vengeance. God is simply saying he is the only one who can handle its power without being overcome by it. Sin can never conquer sin. It is foolish to believe that your sexual sin could do what only Christ's death on the cross could do—bring justice to injustice.

8. **Bitterness (sin as my justice).** When bitterness is our trigger, sin has become our justice. If sin-as-revenge is fast and hot, then sin-as-justice is slow and cold. No longer are we seeking to hurt another by our actions; now we merely nurse our wound. We don't pretend our sin is right or acceptable, but we feel justified because sinning somehow seems to balance the scale of the hurt we've experienced.

   ▶ **Read Hebrews 12:15–17.** In this passage a "root of bitterness" is directly linked to sexual sin (v. 16). When bitterness distorts our perspective, we will trade things of greater value (our integrity) for things of lesser value (a sexual release or fantasy briefly brought to life). We become "like Esau, who sold his birthright for a single meal."

9. **Failure (sin as my success).** When failure is our trigger, sin has become our success. In the fantasy world of sexual sin (porn, romance media, or adultery), you always win. You get the girl. You are the rescued beauty. Real life cannot compete with the seeming success rate of sin. Sin pays up front and costs in the back. Real success costs up front and pays in the back. In healthy marriages, sacrifice is a primary part of joy. If the adulterous relationship is made permanent, it will then become real enough so that it no longer plays by the fantasy rules of success.

   ▶ **Read Matthew 21:28–32.** Why would the second son say, "I go, sir" and not do the assigned task (v. 30)? One possible reason is the fear of failure. When we fear failure, we distance ourselves and become disingenuous with those who have legitimate expectations of us (i.e., spouse, family, accountability partner, etc.). We prefer those that have no claim on us—like pornography because it's a fantasy or an adultery partner because they'll also be found out if they get upset.

10. **Success (sin as my reward).** When success is our trigger, sin has become our reward. Has your sexual sin become your anticipated activity for a break or as your reward for completing a task? Has your sexual sin become the carrot you dangle in front of yourself to maintain motivation? When sin becomes the way we reward ourselves, we feel cheated by repentance. God, and anyone who speaks on his behalf, becomes a killjoy.

> ▶ **Read Hebrews 11:23–28.** Moses was faced with a choice between which reward he believed would be most satisfying: the treasure of Egypt or the privilege of being God's servant (v. 26). Sexual sin gives us a similar reward choice: easy treasure or humble service. Unless Christ is our hero and God is the loving Father we desire to emulate, then the choice seems like a no-brainer in the direction of destruction.

> When sin becomes the way we reward ourselves, we feel cheated by repentance.

11. **Entitlement (sin as my unquestioned right).** When entitlement is our trigger, sin has become like a constitutional right. When confronted with your sexual sin, do you think or say, "How else am I going to get what I need or deserve?" We need to remember that sin is not something to be deserved. Sin is a form of debt, not currency. Whatever benefit it seemingly provides is a form of bondage.

> ▶ **Read Jeremiah 6:15 and 8:12.** The people of God had lost their ability to blush at sin. Why? One explanation is they believed they deserved their sin. When this happens, we believe we know better than God. Our preferences and desires take precedence over the timeless truths of God's created order.

12. **Desire to please (sin as my affirmation).** When the desire to please is our trigger, sin has become our affirmation. It is easy to please a porn star or an adultery partner. They have a vested

interest in being pleased. The entire relationship is based upon commerce ("the customer is always right") or convenience ("if I am not pleasing to you, you have somewhere else to go"), rather than commitment ("I choose you unconditionally and faithfully in good times and in bad"). Too often sexual sin becomes a place of escape when we don't feel like we can make important people in our life happy.

> ▶ **Read Ephesians 4:25–32.** Notice that the type of relational interaction described in these verses is incompatible with an overly strong desire to please others. We cannot live the life God called us to if we are driven by others' affirmation. Our conversation must be gracious and good for building up (v. 29), but that assumes we are willing to speak in ways that may be uncomfortable.

13. **Time of day (sin as regulator).** When time of day is our trigger for sexual sin, sin has become our regulator. Do you use your sexual sin to help you sleep, get the day started, or kill dead time? What common times of day or week do you struggle with sexual sin? When has your sexual sin become part of your routine?

> ▶ **Read 1 Timothy 4:7–10.** When you use sin as a regulator, you are training yourself for ungodliness (the opposite of v. 7). This motive and trigger helps us see the power of habituation in sexual sin. When we use sin as a regulator for our day, it begins to take more intentionality not to sin than to sin.

14. **Negative self-thoughts (sin as my silencer).** When negative self-thoughts are our trigger, sin has become our silencer. In sexual fantasy, we are always desired, and we see ourselves through the eyes of the one desiring us. We give more credence to the passing affirmation of a porn star or our adultery partner than to how God sees us.

> ▶ **Read Psalm 103.** Sin will never do what only God can do. The ultimate silencer of our negative self-thoughts is Christ's death on the cross, which affirms that we were as bad as we thought but replaces our deficiency with his righteousness. Sexual sin

provides fantasy righteousness. It provides the kind of covering mocked in the classic children's book *The Emperor's New Clothes*.

15. **Being in public (sin as my carnival).** When being in public is our trigger, then sin has become our carnival. We walk through life like a kid at an amusement park; gawking at every person we see like a new roller coaster or making a clownish sexual innuendo out of every comment. Our private thoughts of fantasy become fueled by a hypersexualized interpretation of our surroundings.

> You don't have to be in a sexually tempting moment to combat the motives that fuel your sexual sin.

▶ **Read Romans 1:24–25.** Can you hear in the description of sex as a carnival what it means to have "exchanged the truth about God for a lie and worshiped and served the creature rather than the Creator" (v. 25)? God will give us over to this kind of lustful heart (v. 24). This is why radical amputation of sin is a necessary and wise response to prevent sexual sin from becoming our carnival (Matthew 5:27–30).

As you conclude your work on this part of Step 3, list the top five motives and triggers for your sexual sin.

1. _____
   _____
2. _____
   _____
3. _____
   _____
4. _____
   _____
5. _____
   _____

It is important to realize that these distorted motives are present in other areas of your life. That shouldn't be an altogether discouraging statement. Yes, it means our sin is more pervasive than we care to admit. But it also means the opportunities for us to grow and renounce sin are ever present. You don't have to be in a sexually tempting moment to combat the motives that fuel your sexual sin.

As you identify other areas of your life with these distorted motives, realize that you can begin to starve lust in those moments. In a war, armies use direct combat to attack each other's supply chains. When you intentionally counter these motives in moments when sexual temptation is absent, you are essentially battling against the supply chain that fuels your temptation. Use what you've learned about yourself in this part of Step 3 to win battles and make strategic progress in your overall war with sin.

G4 GROUP DISCUSSION: STEP 3, PART TWO

As you discuss this material in G4 group, these questions are meant to facilitate a more honest and beneficial dialogue about this material. Anyone is free to respond to whichever questions they choose.

Experienced Members

- How did seeing the role these motives play in your life help you grow in godliness in areas other than lust?
- Which motive(s) still become easily distorted for you?

New Members

- Which motives stand out as most influential in your life?
- How did it impact you to realize we use sin for purposes that sin can never fulfill?
- How can we pray for you?

Everyone

- How has it been helpful to see triggers and motives as two sides of the same coin?
- Which of the devotionals that accompanied each motive was most impactful for you?
- Have you experienced a significant setback or victory since last meeting that you should tell the group about?

STEP 3
PART THREE

CAPTURING MY PRESENT STRUGGLE

The video for this part of Step 3 can be found at: bradhambrick.com/falselove3p3.

Think about a game between two unevenly matched teams. One team has superior athletes at every position. No one who is informed about the sport—whatever it may be—would pick the inferior team as even having a chance to win. That is often how we feel in our battle against sin. Sin has the home field advantage of our sinful nature and a world full of temptation to go with Satan's predatory nature trying to ensnare us. How can we ever win?

Yet, when movies are made about these kinds of sports battles—think *Hoosiers* or *Miracle*—two things are inevitably true about the underdog that pulls the upset—they know themselves very well, and they have scouted their opponent well. The reality is that the superior team can never win without revealing tendencies and strategies that can help the underdog be victorious. We want to bring Step 3 to a close by introducing a tool to help you get to know yourself and your adversary well during the pivotal moments of temptation.

CAPTURING EACH TEMPTATION IN REAL TIME

The overarching goal of Step 3 is to allow you to see yourself more accurately in real time. When we experience temptation, it is hard to see ourselves and our situation accurately. When our assessment is distorted, it is less likely that our efforts at fleeing temptation will be effective. However, when we slow down enough to assess our situation, what seems impossible becomes possible with God's grace.

The journaling tool that concludes Step 3 is designed to help you do the following two things during each moment of temptation that you experience:

1. Gather the relevant information you've learned to assess during the first three steps. You will notice that sections of this journaling tool are labeled Admit, Acknowledge & Confess, and Understand These sections will help you capture part of your present experience to coincide with the work you've already done.

2. Gather information that will allow you to be better equipped to effectively implement the remaining steps. You will notice that other sections of this tool are labeled Repent and Restructure Life & Implement. As you complete this part of the journal, you are gleaning information for the journey ahead.

A printable PDF of this tool can be found at **bradhambrick.com/falselove**.

PURSUIT OF SEXUAL INTEGRITY JOURNAL

ADMIT:

What was the situation? Summarize the who, what, when, and where of your sexual temptation or sin.

How did I react? Summarize what you thought and felt in the situation.

What lies did you tell before, during, or after your temptation? To whom did you tell these lies?

ACKNOWLEDGE & CONFESS:

What are the consequences? Who was affected by your sin (directly or by changed expectations)?

What forms did your lust take? Circle all that apply

Objectifying People	Private Narrative Lust	Soft Pornography	Hard Pornography
Real Anonymous Person	Emotional Affair	Sexual Touch	Onetime Sexual Encounter
Adultery in Relationship	Pseudo-Spouse	Illegal Sexual Sin	

UNDERSTAND:

What are my motives? Circle or write in your motive/trigger.

Boredom (Sin as Joy)	Loneliness (Sin as Friend)	Stress (Sin as Comforter)	Frustration (Sin as Peace)
Fatigue (Sin as Life)	Hurt (Sin as Refuge)	Betrayal (Sin as Revenge)	Bitterness (Sin as Justice)
Failure (Sin as Success)	Success (Sin as Reward)	Entitlement (Sin as Unquestioned Right)	Desire to Please (Sin as Affirmation)
Time of Day (Sin as Regulator)	Negative Thoughts (Sin as Silencer)	Public (Sin as Carnival)	

Other: _____

REPENT:

How can I turn to God for help? What do repentance and faith look like *now*?

RESTRUCTURE LIFE & IMPLEMENT:

How did I leave myself susceptible to temptation?

Is there anything I am tempted to hide, ignore, or cover up about this temptation?

TALKING TO YOUR MOTIVES

We take the time to identify our motives to start healthier conversations with God, others, and ourselves. In the final part of Step 3, we will look at our internal conversations—that is, self-talk. In Step 4, we will look at our conversations with God, and in Step 5, we will examine our conversations with others.

A large part of overcoming temptation is navigating conversations between your old self and your new self (Ephesians 4:20–24), the spirit and the flesh (Galatians 5:16–24), or your sin nature and your new nature in Christ (Romans 5:12–21). The Bible speaks of this internal battle in many ways. Here are the steps in your basic strategy from this point forward:

> We take the time to identify our motives to start healthier conversations with God, others, and ourselves.

1. Recognize your distorted motives as belonging to your old self, which is bent on destruction.
2. Express faith by doubting the messages of your old self.
3. Challenge the messages of your old self with the truth of what God says about who you are.
4. Make choices that honor God and contribute to your flourishing based upon God's truth.

Realize in this process that you have four options to address the messages from your old self or sinful-flesh nature:

> agree and obey—a worst-case scenario
> disagree and obey—a step in the right direction
> agree and disobey—a further step in the right direction
> disagree and disobey—our desired destination for being healthy and free

These four options are represented in the chart below. This chart demonstrates that you do not have to condemn yourself for hearing the destructive messages of your flesh. Instead, your goal is simply to disagree and disobey your flesh. The part of you that clings to these destructive messages will slowly be put to death through faith and obedience. Don't allow a sense of condemnation over your flesh's continued presence to strengthen your flesh through guilt, shame, or a sense of failure.

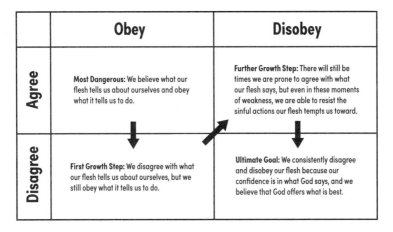

Figure 3. Talking to Your Motives

Here is a sample of how your inner dialogue and actions might change from quadrant to quadrant. When using this exercise, take these generic statements and tailor them to the motive–trigger behind your temptation and the specific sins your flesh is tempting you to perform.

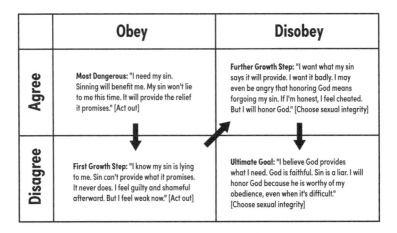

Figure 4. Talking to Your Motives: Sample

Pick one of the dominant motives for your addiction and fill in the chart below with what your internal dialogue is likely to sound like as you grow into the freedom God has for you.

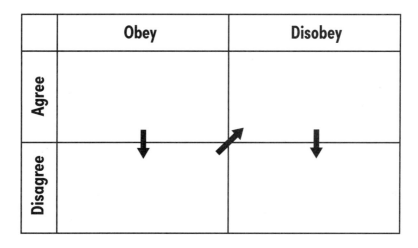

Use this chart to help you identify what your options are in moments of temptation. Take the time to articulate your four choices. Resist the urge to feel rushed by your temptation. Articulating your options not only makes the best choice clear, but it also puts you in the frame of mind to enact that choice. In times of temptation, call a friend in your support network and use this chart to acquaint them with your inner struggle.

This four-quadrant exercise is included with the printable PDF journaling tool.

CONCLUSION

Our adversary is daunting. We shouldn't minimize that. But now you have tools to begin scouting your temptation. Whereas before you likely felt powerless in the face of temptation, now your temptation will be unable to manifest without you gathering important information that will become part of the remedy.

More than this, you have a team. Before coming to G4 you were isolated. If temptation were a basketball game, you would have been playing one-on-five. Now you have a group of people supporting you. In addition to a tool for gathering useful information, you now have people to discuss that information with, people who can encourage you. That is a major difference.

The battle may still be hard, but the momentum is shifting in your favor. Press on!

G4 GROUP DISCUSSION: STEP 3, PART THREE

As you discuss this material in G4 group, these questions are meant to facilitate a more honest and beneficial dialogue about this material. Anyone is free to respond to whichever questions they choose.

> You do not have to condemn yourself for hearing the destructive messages of your flesh. Instead, your goal is simply to disagree and disobey your flesh.

Experienced Members

- In what ways did you find the journaling tool of Step 3 helpful? When was it less helpful than you hoped it would be?
- How have you grown in enacting this principle: You do not have to condemn yourself for hearing the destructive messages of your flesh. Instead, your goal is simply to disagree and disobey?

New Members

- In your battle with temptation, how have you felt like the weaker team that gets blown out?
- How did the four-quadrant chart give you a more effective way to talk to these motives?
- How can we pray for you?

Everyone

- What are the advantages to personifying your old self motives so that you talk to them more than embrace them?
- What are the most important things you've learned about yourself and your temptation in Step 3?
- Have you experienced a significant setback or victory since last meeting that you should tell the group?

STEP 4
REPENT TO GOD for how my sin replaced and misrepresented him.

At the end of this step, I want to be able to say . . .

"My sin is a counterfeit god offering an empty salvation. I am beginning to see why my sin is offensive to God as well as the folly of trying to replace God with my sin. I repent not merely because my sin hurts other people and disrupts my life, but because God is superior to my sin, offers a superior salvation, and lovingly enables me to love him (1 John 4:19)."

STEP 4

PART ONE

TO WHOM ARE YOU REPENTING?

The video for this part of Step 4 can be found at: bradhambrick.com/falselove4p1.

As you start Step 4, you probably feel like your soul has been laid bare. Honesty is freeing, but it initially stings like the healing ointment placed on a wound. You have been more honest about yourself, your behaviors, and your life than ever before. In Step 4, you are going to bring that honesty to God. You are not bringing God information that he needs to act on your behalf. You are placing yourself in a position to receive what God has already done and has always been willing to do on your behalf.

If you presume upon God's forgiveness, you are not repenting. Those thoughts might look like this: "God has to forgive me because he's already sent Jesus to die. It would be a waste if he didn't follow through. Besides, God would be a liar if he promised to forgive and didn't honor his word. I'll go through the ritual to get what's coming to me if that is what he wants." In this case, you are making a legal transaction with someone you believe to be too foolish to know better. Additionally, you are leveraging God's grace in a manipulative fashion against others— that is "If God has forgiven me, why can't you?" If this fits you, receive the strong warning of Galatians 6:7, "God is not mocked."

If you neglect seeking God's forgiveness, then you are wallowing in self-pity and will remain in the same shame cycle that has likely fueled your sexual sin for a long time. Those thoughts might look like this: "I don't deserve to be forgiven. I should have to pay for what I've done wrong. I've made enough people suffer because of my selfishness, so I shouldn't add Jesus to the list." You would remain a relationally unsafe person who will use self-pity to manipulate others with guilt.

The only way out of sin is through genuine repentance because all lasting change is built upon repentance. Our repentance changes our primary allegiance from self to God. In repentance, we turn from trusting our ways to trusting God's ways. In repentance, our primary goals changes from self-satisfaction and self-protection to glorifying God and loving others.

Repentance requires laying down our pride. Pride says, "I don't have a problem . . . I don't need help . . . I can do this on my own . . . I know what I need to do . . . Other people trying to help is a nuisance . . . I'm not like *those people* who struggle with sexual sin." Repentance is laying down our pride and embracing the grace found in Jesus Christ.

▶ **Read Proverbs 3:34, James 4:6, and 1 Peter 5:5.** A common response to these passages is "Okay already, I get the point." God repeats himself when we are prone to ignore, resist, or think we don't need his message. And this is one of the most repeated messages in Scripture. There is always more grace for the humble, but the proud march face-first into the chest of God, disgruntled that anyone—including God—would get in their way. How will you ever gain the strength to sustain the changes that are ahead? It requires humbling yourself so you can receive the perpetually available supply of God's grace.

Step 4 solidifies all the work you have done to this point and serves as the foundation for each step remaining on your journey. You have learned a great deal about yourself and your sin in the first three steps. It would be tempting to think this information would help you master and conquer your sexual sin. But in repentance, we commit to quit trying to make our broken ways work and trying to do life in our own strength. Instead, we rely more fully and joyfully on the God we trust more than ourselves.

TO WHOM ARE YOU REPENTING?

The identity of God is a significant point of controversy in Christian recovery circles. The generic "God of your understanding" referred to in Alcoholics Anonymous (AA) rightly makes many Christians uncomfortable. However, suggesting that God can be anything we want him to be departs significantly from the way AA founder Bill Wilson (the basis for SA on sexual addiction), originally used the phrase. The original usage was meant to be an expression of humility, not universalism. Bill Wilson recognized that he, like all of us, had many misconceptions about God, and that as he pursued God, these misconceptions would need to be progressively corrected. None of us has a completely accurate view of God when we first come to faith. We reach out to God as we understand him at that time. As in any relationship, the depth and accuracy of our knowledge grows with time.

In this G4 material, we do not believe all conceptions of deity are equal. We believe there is one true God who stepped into time as the second member of the Trinity, Jesus Christ. He lived the life we were supposed to live, died the death our sin deserves, and is scandalously willing to offer us his righteousness for our surrender. Talking to any other god is a form of talking to ourselves and has the power of talking to a doorknob or a chair.

> The only way out of sin is through genuine repentance because all lasting change is built upon repentance.

All of this to say that what you believe about God matters. It doesn't just matter theologically, as if life was about passing a seminary quiz. It matters practically. What you believe about God will determine whether you reach out to him for help and how you engage with him if you do.

In this section, we will look at common misconceptions about God that hinder our willingness to turn from our sexual sin toward God's care. Correcting these misunderstandings is more than an intellectual exercise. It is about cultivating trust more than learning facts. Placing an increasing amount of emotional weight on these truths takes time.

Knowing God is more than knowing propositions—that is, God is all powerful, God is all knowing, etc. Having a relationship with a president is different from knowing their name, hair color, and hometown. As you build a more accurate understanding of who God is, you will find your prayers becoming more personal and conversational. That doesn't mean you've been placing the wrong mailing address on your prayers, but that your knowledge of the person who lived at that address was skewed. God receives our prayers even when we don't know him very well.

The one you pray to is more important than the words in your prayer. Too often we are not praying to the one true God who made us with a purpose and loves us beyond measure (Ephesians 2:8–10). Too often we think our words must convince a stingy deity to be generous with us. Too often we believe that God is only paying attention to our lives when we mess up.

> What comes into our minds when we think about God is the most important thing about us. The history of mankind will probably show that no people has ever risen above its religion, and man's spiritual history will positively demonstrate that no religion has ever been greater than its idea of God. . . . We tend by a secret law of the soul to move toward our mental image of God. . . . The most [determining] fact about any man is not what he at a given time may say or do, but what he in his deep heart conceives God to be like. —A. W. Tozer[1]

In this section, we want to debunk **five misconceptions about God** that make repentance seem either powerless or punitive. When we don't know God accurately or rely on him fully, then other areas of life—like our sexual sin—will necessarily begin to try to fill a role that is too large for them.

1. **God as not enough.** We often do not repent from our sexual sin because we find God to be less desirable than our sin. We only repent when we value the relationship with the one to whom we are repenting more than the perceived gain from our sin. If our conviction to repent is low, this means the value we place on our relationship with God is also low. Consider this quote from *Mere Christianity*:

   > All that we call human history—money, poverty, ambition, war, prostitution, classes, empires, slavery—[is] the long terrible story of man trying to find something other than God which will make him happy. —C. S. Lewis[2]

   This is why repentance must begin with a great love for God rather than an intense sorrow for sin (in the end both are required). Without a great love for God, when life begins to improve, our repentance will wane because our desire was relief from guilt rather than a restored relationship with God.

> The fire of lust's pleasures must be fought with the fire of God's pleasures. If we try to fight the fire of lust with prohibitions and threats alone—even the terrible warnings of Jesus—we will fail. We must fight it with a massive promise of superior happiness. We must swallow up the little flicker of lust's pleasure in the conflagration of holy satisfaction. —John Piper[3]

We often buy into the "God as not enough" lie through attempts at self-forgiveness to resolve our guilt. It is common to hear people say, "I know God has forgiven me, but I just can't forgive myself." The implication is that God's forgiveness comes at a cheaper price than our own. We turn to ourselves for the ultimate and final forgiveness that frees us from our burden of guilt. In guilt, we become our own god in comparable ways to trying to become the center of the universe in our sexual sin.[4]

> The one you pray to is more important than the words in your prayer.

> Why is this so hard? It is because your natural instinct is to turn to yourself, instead of to Jesus. Sexual sins are all about you: what you want, what you hope for, and what you long for. When you are facing hard or disappointing circumstances—boredom, loneliness, money problems, fighting with a spouse, distance from a friend—it's easy (and instinctive) to turn in on yourself. . . . After you sin, it's easy (and instinctive) to stay turned in on yourself, but in a different way. Now, because you feel guilty, you chew on yourself, kick yourself, and are dismayed with yourself. But even your guilt is all about you. Your only hope for deliverance from this never-ending cycle of turning in on yourself is to go out to Jesus. —David Powlison[5]

Finally, we believe the lie "God as not enough" when our sexual sin has deceived us into confusing "God is love" (1 John 4:8, 16) with "God is lust." We begin to view lust and sexual gratification as ultimate. We lose sight of what real love is. One of Satan's primary tactics has always been to masquerade as God's messenger (2 Corinthians 11:14).

This is especially true in prolonged adultery relationships where people often say they are in love and ask, "Would God want me to remain in an unhappy marriage?" The question screams of self-centered sin-blindness. The tables have been turned to the point that they now believe that God exists for their happiness rather than people existing for God's glory.

The following is a paraphrase of a fictional story told by C. S. Lewis in *The Great Divorce*. It captures both the self-deception of sexual sin and the relationship that exists between love and lust. As you read it, realize that repenting will require you to die to self in ways that are painful. Sin sets its roots and talons in our life and makes no plans to leave. But repentance is a good gift from a good God who offers us a better life than the bondage of sin.

The soul of a man afflicted by lust is about to enter hell. In this fictional story, lust is personified as a red lizard sitting on the man's shoulder and whispering in his ear. We're not sure what is said, but in a moment of clarity, the man sees the lizard for what it is—a messenger of Satan—and is angry at the lizard. As clarity emerges, an angel from heaven appears and offers to kill the red lizard.

The man is torn between loving his lust and wanting lust to die. Part of the man so loves the lizard that he fears killing the lizard (i.e., lust) will kill him. As the man deliberates, the angel continues to ask, "Will you allow me to kill it?" The man starts making excuses, saying that he'll manage the lizard better, but finally, he agrees to let the angel destroy the lizard. Once lust is killed, the ghostly man is gloriously remade into a real and solid human. But instead of decaying, the lizard is transformed into a white stallion, representing actual love. The man mounts the horse, and they ride to heaven.[6]

In this story, C. S. Lewis shows the connection between killing lust and embracing life. Repentance feels like it will destroy us. But that is another of Satan's lies. Instead, when lust is forsaken, we become more alive, not less. We become more of a real person with a greater capacity for real relationships with other real people. You are repenting to the God who makes you whole.

2.   **God as unemotional.** We may avoid repenting because we think God is more concerned about what we've done than what we're going through. It feels as if God is only concerned about our sin and disregards the suffering our sin created. Our expectation of God's response to our repentance is that he will sarcastically say, "What did you think was going to happen?"

But think about the way your sexual sin impacts you and those you love (Step 2). Would God be loving if he was content for you to multiply these effects? God is concerned about your sin because it is multiplying your suffering by putting distance between you and him. God couldn't love you and be content for you to remain enslaved to sexual sin.

God wants to bring comfort to the parts of your history that contribute to your sexual sin (history components of Steps 2 and 3), but you must trust him enough to forsake your self-destruction before you can experience his comfort.

> ▶ **Read Hebrews 2:14–18.** Notice that Jesus's compassion is central to the gospel message. God was not merely concerned to pay the full price for our sin so that we could get into heaven (i.e., propitiation). God was also very concerned that we know he understands our struggles so that we would want to be near him. Heaven is not meant to be an eternal all-inclusive vacation where there is so much to enjoy that we never get bored; heaven is about being with the One our heart desires, God himself. The gospel must contain this kind of emotional and relational concern.

Do this thought experiment: Review your full disclosure. Imagine reading it to God as a prayer. Now, in your mind's eye, look up. What expression is on God's face? Is he angry or compassionate; frustrated with you or concerned for you? Read the end of Hebrews 2 again. Does your instinctual response accurately represent God?

3. **God as irrelevant.** "Okay, so God cares, but how can he actually help me? God's not going to make my sexual longings disappear. God's not going to instantly change my brain so that it doesn't crave self-gratification. Doesn't even understanding that God cares still leave everything up to me and my choices?"

Yes and no. God won't change you against your will. God is a gentleman and will not force himself upon you. In that sense, everything is up to you and your choices. But *relationships enhance the number of choices that are available to us.* In isolation, you have the choices that your strength, wisdom, or abilities provide. When it's just you, it's your desire to be pure against your sexual desires. Good intentions are simply that—intentions to do what we know we should do until what we want to do trumps wisdom. When it's just you, it's your word against your word. It is your voice, "I'm bored . . . hurting . . . worthless," competing with your voice, "I know sexual sin will only make it worse."

When God enters our picture, healthy and happy no longer need to compete because God's voice can serve as the final, loving arbiter between our fickle desires. This doesn't mean we can't choose what is destructive, but it does mean we have more options than we did when we were alone and that we can use God's strength to pursue those options.

> ▶ **Read Matthew 11:28–30.** In this passage, Jesus represents us as weary oxen carrying a load too great for us. He offers to share that yoke—the piece of wood fashioned to connect two oxen to a plow. God offers to come alongside us to give his strength to our toils and to guide the process. It was customary practice in biblical times to pair an inexperienced ox with an experienced one so that the older ox could guide the younger one to plow straight rows. God's relevance does not eliminate the necessity for us to walk out the change process, but God offers needed strength and direction for a task that is too great for our strength.

4. **God as unpleasable.** If you view God as having standards that you are unable to meet, you may give up. You may say to yourself, "I won't ever do it good enough for God. After all, doesn't God

require perfection? There is no way I am going to be completely pure every day for the rest of my life. I get that God is beside me, but I know me. I'll stray even with a yoke connecting me to God. I'm an expert at wandering."

It may be helpful to think of repentance as a commitment rather than a promise. God makes promises. He can keep them. We make commitments. Our repentance is not a promise never to fail again, but instead a perpetually renewed commitment to follow God and what he designed to be satisfying for our lives. When you talk about your struggle with sexual sin, speak of your commitment to this G4 journey rather than a promise to never do "that" again.

Realize that God is pleased with progress as much as perfection. When God designed the Christian life, he decided to transform our character over time, which theologians call "progressive sanctification." This was God's idea and not a concession he made because we couldn't do any better. God, as the epitome of a good Father, delights in the maturation of his children over time. He loves being part of the growth process.

> ► **Read Hebrews 10:14.** Contrast the verb tenses. The ESV says God "has perfected" (past completed action) those who are "being sanctified" (ongoing action). This is not a contradiction, but rather a picture. Why isn't God displeased enough with your failures to give up on you? He knows what he has already done in you. Why is God still calling you to faith and obedience? This is how he brings to fruition what he has already guaranteed. As you faithfully—yet imperfectly—follow God, he faithfully and perfectly keeps his promise.

5. **God as unapproachable.** Until you come to him, all these truths about God are merely nice thoughts. We must approach God or we are alone with our sin. God is compassionate, relevant, and able to be pleased in Christ. However, you must come to him.

   To repent with confidence, we must believe that God delights in forgiving and being restored to his children. God hates sin because it destroys the life of his beloved children. We must also understand that what our Bible says about sin speaks to our specific sin. Consider the following biblical passage from Romans 8 paraphrased by Tim Chester. Allow it to be shockingly uncomfortable and change your view of God from angrily unapproachable to a loving Father deeply desiring his children to accept his invitation for restoration.

> Romans 8:3–4, "For God has done what the law, weakened by the flesh, could not do. By sending his own Son in the likeness of sinful flesh and for sin, he condemned sin in the flesh, in order that the righteous requirement of the law might be fulfilled in us, who walk not according to the flesh but according to the Spirit."
>
> For what the law was powerless to do in that is was weakened by the sinful nature, God did by sending his own Son in the likeness of porn users to be an offering for the sin of porn. And so he condemned the sin of porn in sinful man, in order that the requirements of sexual purity might be fully met in us, who do not live according to the sinful nature but according to the Spirit. (Romans 8:3–4 paraphrased, Tim Chester)[7]

This is where many people pull up short. They learn many things about God. They learn how God feels about them and what he's done to make a renewed relationship with him possible. But they don't come to him. For some, this is failing to come to God for saving-faith (initial salvation). For others, it is a failure to come to God for sustaining faith (the ongoing battle with indwelling sin). Either way, information is mistaken for relationship.

Think of a child with a favorite sports hero. The child could tell you that player's every statistic and piece of life history. But they have information, not a relationship. If that player was the child's father, they would play catch, shoot baskets, get ice cream, cry, ask questions, and just hang out. That would be a relationship. Have you brought *all* your life—not only your sexual sin—to God in this way?

> ▶ **Read Hebrews 4:14–16.** Underline the phrase "with confidence draw near" (or the equivalent in your translation). Does this describe your relationship with God? God intends

to be supremely approachable. If you did not have parents who were approachable in this way, it may feel odd to have this kind of father–child relationship with God. But don't allow that lack of familiarity to prevent you from embracing what God offers. Repentance is not punishment; it's not God putting you in time-out to think about what you did. Rather, repentance is God's provision to restore the relationship he always intended to have with you.

► **Read Romans 2:4.** Notice that it is the kindness of God that brings us to repentance. This is what accounts for the sense of risk we feel. The outcome is guaranteed; God has already promised forgiveness. We hesitate not because we doubt the offer, but because we doubt the character of the one making the offer. Before moving to the next section on the key elements of repentance, realize that your ability to have this conversation will be directly proportional to how much you trust the character of the One with whom you're speaking.

► **Reflection:** How has this section challenged your view of God? How is God different from what you imagined him to be?

One of the main goals for this section has been to reduce the shame often associated with sexual sin. We often fail to deal with the guilt of our sin through repentance because we are paralyzed by shame. Reflect on the following points to differentiate shame from guilt and regret:

- Guilt is a sense of *legitimate condemnation* in response to sin. God resolves guilt through forgiveness, and we access God's remedy through repentance.
- Shame can be a *sense of identity* we take on as we allow our sin to define us. God resolves this type of shame by providing us with an identity greater than our sin, and we access God's remedy by continually embracing this new identity. Self-deprecating statements are a sign we're living out of our old shame-based identity.
- Shame can be a *sense of illegitimate condemnation* in response to suffering. God resolves this type of shame with

comfort and acceptance, and we access God's remedy by entrusting God with our sorrows (Matthew 5:4). Fleeing to sexual sin is often an alternative and empty remedy for this type of shame.

- Regret is a form of grief for a reasonable, good circumstance that was never realized. Sexual sin introduces many regret-based griefs into our lives. God promises that the sweetness of future obedience is greater than the bitterness of past regret. We realize God's promise is true when we grieve our regrets without allowing them to distract us from obedience.

As you get to know God, grow in your comfort to approach God for resolution to guilt, shame, and regret. The best sexual sin can offer for these emotions is a temporary distraction that only makes the problem worse. Embrace the freedom from these painful emotions that God wants for you.

G4 GROUP DISCUSSION: STEP 4, PART ONE

As you discuss this material in G4 group, these questions are meant to facilitate a more honest and beneficial dialogue about this material. Anyone is free to respond to whichever questions they choose.

Experienced Members

- How has your relationship to honesty changed over the course of your G4 journey?
- How has your prayer life and view of God changed over the course of your G4 journey?

New Members

- Which of the five common misconceptions about God creates the most interference for you?
- When you think about talking to God about your sexual sin, what expression is on his face?
- How can we pray for you?

Everyone

- How have you seen the truth of the statement "relationships enhance the number of choices that are available to us" during your G4 journey?
- Which devotional about the common misconceptions about God was most clarifying for you? What difference has this more accurate view of God made in your G4 journey?
- Have you experienced a significant setback or victory since the last meeting that you should tell the group?

STEP 4
PART TWO

WHAT IS REPENTANCE?

The video for this part of Step 4 can be found at: bradhambrick.com/falselove4p2.

There is no formula for repentance. It is not an incantation that only works if we say all the hocus-pocus, mumbo-jumbo words just right. It is not like ordering the perfect coffee from a barista. Instead, repentance is about restoring a relationship. Repentance is like saying "I love you," and there are many ways to communicate that sentiment.

TRAITS OF TRUE REPENTANCE

God has already told us that he loves us. Repentance is our opportunity to say it back. In addition, repentance will free us from the shame and guilt associated with our sin. The six points below are meant to help you experience the full redemptive impact of repentance. In this sense, repentance and God's forgiveness can be like a smartphone. When we buy the phone, we get all the features, but we do not get the full benefit of them until we realize they're there and learn how to utilize them.

Following each point, we offer self-assessment questions, which are meant to help you determine whether you are placing yourself in a position to receive the benefits God intends to provide through repentance.

1. **A desire to live for God and submit to his lordship.** Repentance does not begin with remorse. If that were the case, then we would say the cure for guilt begins with feeling worse. Repentance begins with a genuine desire to submit to God's lordship because we trust God's character. Repentance begins with the belief that what God wants for us is what is best. We trust God to lead our lives more than we trust ourselves.

> They [those trapped in sexual sin] like to think they
> are in control, but they are not. Indeed, their inability
> to give up the illusion of control is precisely what pre-
> vents sex addicts from healing. It is the same with any
> sin. Our attempts to control our lives prevent us from
> trusting God to care for us. —Mark Laaser[1]

When we see God's ways are best, we are sorry we strayed from
God's ways, not just sad about the consequences of our actions. This
remorse is not distasteful like shame; instead, it is like the reunion with
a trusted friend after you realize you were wrongly upset with them
and they graciously embrace the friendship again.

> ▶ **Self-Assessment:** Are you surrendering to the lordship of
> Christ because you trust his love for you, or are you only
> seeking relief from destructive habits?

2. **An understanding of how our sin sought to replace God.** It is not
   just actions or distorted motives for which we repent. We repent
   for having replaced God with our sin. Look back at Step 3. Recall
   how the motives for sexual sin fill every role that God should fill
   in our lives.

   The idols that fuel our sin want to control all our lives—
   to interpret all the events and people in our lives. Repentance
   acknowledges this false worship as an affront to God and wants
   him to have his rightful place in our lives and to properly interpret
   the events and people in our lives.

   > ▶ **Self-Assessment:** Were you able to see the God-replacing
   > nature of your sin? How did these idols distort the way you
   > interpreted people and events in your life?

3. **A brokenness over the nature of our sin.** A healthy life begins
   with recognizing our fallen human condition. Ultimately, we sin
   because we are sinners. The myriad of factors that led to our sin
   are not the root cause. The root cause is that our nature has been
   distorted by the fall (1 Corinthians 15:21–22).

   True repentance is not just sorrow over our idols or behaviors,
   but brokenness over our condition as a sinful person. When we

acknowledge our depravity, we gain an accurate self-assessment that motivates us to perpetually rely on God. Realizing that repentance is the perpetual need of every person allows honesty that is not based in shame.

> Here are three common reasons why people want to kick their porn habit: (1) to prove ourselves to God—so he will bless us or save us; (2) to prove ourselves to other people—so people like us or approve of us; (3) to prove ourselves to ourselves—so we feel good about ourselves . . . None of these reasons works, because they put "me" at the center of my change project. And putting myself at the center is pretty much the definition of sin! —Tim Chester[2]

Repentance allows you not to be either fake or fatalistic about your shortcomings and ongoing struggles. Repentance allows you to be honest and have hope at the same time.

> ▶ **Self-Assessment:** Do you resist seeing yourself and allowing yourself to be known as someone who is in perpetual need of God's sustaining grace?

4. **An expression to God.** After sin, our pride or fear causes us to hide from God rather than talk to him (Genesis 3:8). Too often we think that a directionless sense of regret for sin is the same thing as repenting to God. That's not repentance; it's wallowing. It's not a conversation; it's a shame-based reflection.

   You will not feel restored to God if you avoid him because of your sin. It does no good to address your repentance "to whom it may concern." Any ambiguously addressed repentance is little more than talking to yourself. When you repent, talk to God so that you can gain his response to your repentance.

   > ▶ **Self-Assessment:** Have you talked to God in your repentance? If not, might your repentance seem ineffective because the "no one" you spoke to has no power to forgive or comfort?

5. **A belief in God's willingness to forgive.** Repentance is an expression of faith. We come to God with nothing to offer in exchange for

our forgiveness. If we do not believe God will freely forgive, we will continue in trying harder or hiding more effectively, which allows our sexual sin to fester. All this does is inadvertently reinforce the false beliefs that our sin is good and God is mean. Unless we believe that God is willing to forgive because of his grace and Christ's death, repentance becomes a form of penance that is more like putting peace in layaway than receiving a gift. The following testimony describes such a cycle:

> Repentance allows you to be honest and have hope at the same time.

> I went through that cycle a thousand times: the excitement of sin, the misery, and then the craving would come back. It was intoxicatingly powerful because it was more than just sex. It was worship, self-worship. But Jesus Christ is more powerful. Once I got honest, I found grace. —Anonymous testimony in David Powlison's *Pornography: Slaying the Dragon*[3]

> ▶ **Self-Assessment:** How do you view God when you come to him in repentance? How has it changed since you began your work on Step 4?

6. **A new direction of life that begins with confession.** This will be clarified more in Steps 5 and 6. For now, think of repentance like marriage. Repentance is entering (or recommitting to) a covenant relationship with God. This is why sin is frequently called spiritual adultery (James 4:4).

Repentance is our vow-renewal ceremony that expresses our renewed commitment to covenant fidelity. Marriage ceremonies and vow renewals are not done in private. They are public declarations of where our ultimate allegiance lies. This parallels why repentance doesn't remain private. It is also expressed through confession (Step 5).

> ▶ **Self-Assessment:** Does it startle you to think of repentance as a vow-renewal ceremony? How does that image extend the implications of repentance beyond the moment of prayer?

A LIFESTYLE OF REPENTANCE

▶ **Reflection:** Do you think of repentance as an event or a process?

In fact, it is both an event and a process. This is vital to understand on your G4 journey. When we think of repentance as only an event, we are prone to believe that "we repented and it didn't work," when we continue to struggle with sin. How we come to faith—the event of giving our life to Christ—is also how we grow in faith—the lifestyle of repentance. We don't need Christ any less after our salvation than we did before our salvation. Whether you have been a Christian for decades or are still considering whether to give your life to Christ, this is important to understand.

> Too often we think that a directionless sense of regret for sin is the same thing as repenting to God. That's not repentance; it's wallowing.

People should repent, change their ways, and get right with God. I always agree with these statements. The sexual behaviors that become addictive are sinful. . . . Repentance, behavior change, and a deeper relationship with God are all goals of the healing journey for the sex addict. I usually respond to this question with another question: How long do you expect repentance and change to take? —Mark Laaser[4]

As you reflect on the sample prayer in the next section, don't think of it as an outline of a speech (single event) that you need to perform once before God to get him back on your team. Instead, think of it as a conversation (an ongoing process) that you will have with God daily as your relationship with him deepens.

A SAMPLE PRAYER OF REPENTANCE

There is no magic in these words or this outline. The intent is to help you assimilate what you've learned to this point in your journey in a conversation of repentance with God before you begin having confessional conversations with people (Step 5).

As you talk with God, review your notes from previous steps and verbalize what you have learned. Know that God is interested in what you say, not because you have finally learned your lesson but simply because he cares for you (1 Peter 5:7).

Heavenly Father,

I am glad I can come to you amid my sin. I have been hesitant to come to you, because . . .

> *[Describe your misconceptions about God and/or repentance.]*

I also haven't wanted to admit the full extent of my sin—to myself or to you.

> *[Describe what you saw about yourself in Steps 1 and 2.]*

I am beginning to see that the things that have become more important than you—the idols—are fueling sin without providing the relief they promise.

> *[List your motives from Step 3 and describe how you have lived for them.]*

You know how those things came to be so precious to me. You know what I need (Matthew 6:8). Where my desires are good, I trust you to provide. Where my desires are bad or excessive, I ask that you change me in whatever ways are necessary.

> *[Talk about how this scares or confuses you.]*

I have replaced you in my life with my fears and desires. I have declared myself more capable of caring for me than you. I see how wrong and foolish that is. Please forgive me.

> *[Talk with God about the six elements of forgiveness.]*

Thank you for loving me and walking with me through these
unsettling emotions (Psalm 23). I look forward to learning more
about your character as I strive to trust and rely on you more in
my daily life. Lord, grant me the perseverance to continue this
journey even when I'm emotionally weary. Although this road
with you may be hard, the side roads without you are harder. I
know this. Help me not to forget it. Amen.

G4 GROUP DISCUSSION: STEP 4, PART TWO

As you discuss this material in G4 group, these questions are meant
to facilitate a more honest and beneficial dialogue about this material.
Anyone is free to respond to whichever questions they choose.

Experienced Members

- How has your view of repentance changed in your pursuit of
  integrity?
- How has repentance helped you escape the pattern of being
  fake or fatalistic about your sin?

New Members

- How is this depiction of repentance different from what you
  expected?
- Do you talk with God as honestly and conversationally as the
  sample prayer of repentance demonstrates?
- How can we pray for you?

Everyone

- Which of the six marks of repentance is currently most chal-
  lenging for you?
- How has understanding that repentance is both an event and a
  process aided your growth?
- Have you experienced a significant setback or victory since last
  meeting that you should tell the group?

STEP 5
CONFESS TO THOSE AFFECTED
for harm done, and seek
to make amends.

At the end of this step, I want to be able to say to others . . .

"I have not represented God well in your presence.
[List ways your actions misrepresented God's
character.] You have been hurt by my ungodly
actions, attitudes, and beliefs. [List ways this person
has been hurt by you.] My goal in life is to make God's
character known. That starts with this request for
forgiveness. I value our relationship more than my
pride. I am currently working on submitting my life
to God's control, and I understand if you need time
to consider my request for forgiveness."

STEP 5
PART ONE

TO WHOM SHOULD YOU CONFESS?

The video for this part of Step 5 can be found at: bradhambrick.com/falselove5p1.

Y ou will only be as free as you are honest. Privacy kills change and fuels sin. Transparency kills sin and fuels change. Chances are this step may scare you as much as any step you have taken since Step 1. But remember, it is not nearly as scary to move forward as it is dangerous to go backward. Don't allow fear to make you forgetful.

Our tendency has been to face difficult situations through escape and avoidance. That can no longer be our life pattern. Now we will face hardship by being honest. This honesty through confession serves two functions:

1. Acknowledging how we've harmed relationships, seeking forgiveness, and making amends.
2. Inviting people to become a more informed part of our support network.

Confession invites other people into our lives and points out where they can help. It is how we acknowledge our weaknesses and admit that we need their help. We won't lie, dismiss, or lash out. Confession ensures others that we have the humility and realistic expectations necessary to receive help. The time we've spent minimizing and blame-shifting gives our friends and family appropriate caution about whether we can own our sin, but our healthy confession demonstrates that we won't again use our loved one's good intentions toward us against them.

We begin to realize that confession is the door to community—the door through which we must pass if we do not want to be alone in the dark with our sin. In Step 5, we will begin the process of making our community outside G4 as authentic as our community inside G4.

TO WHOM SHOULD WE CONFESS?

Let's state the obvious: Confession is going to make you uncomfortable. Don't allow yourself to become defensive and reply, "I'm not telling everybody my business." That is a fearful exaggeration. Wisdom regulates how far you expand your circle of confession, but even wise confession will make you uncomfortable. Yet confession is necessary if you want to overcome your sin.

> You will only be as free as you are honest. Transparency kills sin and fuels change.

> There is only one thing that clearly is universal: those committed to ruthless honesty consistently overcome their sin and make great strides in holiness. In stark contrast, I have never encountered an individual that overcame sexual struggles if they were unwilling to bring their sin fully into the light, with an ever-increasing number of individuals. Those who refuse this path of ruthless honesty stay stuck in their sin or return to it after a short period of "white-knuckled" abstinence. —David White[1]

Your Spouse

If you disclosed incomplete information or minimized your sex sin, now is the time to fully disclose it to your spouse. But this confession to your spouse should not primarily be new facts. By the time you reach Step 5, your spouse should not be receiving new information. Instead, confession in Step 5 is about your new heart or new disposition toward what your spouse knows.

Between Step 1 and Step 4 you may have been defensive, apathetic, or wallowing in sorrow as you spoke about your sin with your spouse. When our sin comes to light, it often creates emotionally overwhelming circumstances where we feel like we're just trying to survive rather than thinking about how to care for our spouse. For a season, that may have been natural—but natural should not be confused with acceptable, as if your spouse should overlook these reactions. Now that season should be ending.

In Part Two of Step 5, you will begin to put words to this new dis-position. Confession focuses on acknowledging and being sympathetic toward the dominoes of your sin as much as naming your sin. Realize that your spouse may not be ready to hear what you are ready to share. As an act of other-minded love, you should pace your sharing accord-ing to your spouse's readiness. That way, not only *what* you share but also *how* you share it reveals that you are becoming an increasingly safe source of support for your spouse, and they will realize you are sturdy enough to compassionately hear the impact of your sin in their life.

If your spouse is still cautious about you being a source of support for them, honor that. Accepting their hesitancy is a form of acknowl-edging the pain you caused. Your patience is the most effective way to demonstrate that you understand the pain you have caused.

▶ **Read 1 Peter 4:17–19.** God begins judgment with his house-hold. God focuses his attention first where there is the greatest responsibility to know and live by the truth. We should follow this pattern in our confession. We begin where we have the great-est responsibility to live with integrity. Further, confession should begin with those to whom you most want to be restored. This is why we put Step 4 (repentance to God) ahead of Step 5 (confess-ing to others). As we begin Step 5, we maintain the same mindset of prioritizing primary relationships. That is why we recommend having your first confession conversations with those closest to you. If you are married, that includes your spouse.

Your Close Friends

We slid deeper into sin because we hid it from those who truly cared about us. In effect, we trusted our sin more than we trusted our friends. It is time for that to change. Your Christian friends need an awareness of your struggles in order to fulfill the function in your life that God designed for them.

The only way to combat your fears about confession is to confess to your friends. Until you have experienced confession gone well, your imagination will create scenarios of misery and scorn. Until we obey God in a particular area of life, our imaginations are limited by our sin and fears (Psalm 34:8).

Which friends outside your G4 group should you confess to? Confess to friends in each of the following three sets of people. There may be some overlap, but you want to make sure each area is covered.

- **Your small group**. At your church, this group may be called Sunday school, missional communities, or something else, but you get the idea. It is a group who meets together weekly for Bible study, prayer, and community. Confiding in a group like this ensures you have a weekly accountability time that fits with the expectations of the relationship. Currently, your G4 group fills this role. As you look to graduate from G4, the baton for this role will need to be passed to a new group setting. Initially, you would do this with the same-gender members of your small group. If you and your spouse desire mutual support and both are ready, you could share together with the whole group.

- **Your best friend**. The values you instill in your closest relationship will significantly impact your life. Openly emphasizing integrity in your closest friendships is an important way to marinate your life in these virtues. Growing in integrity is not something we should sequester to a private or therapeutic sector of our life. If you need help developing meaningful friendships, consider reading the book *Transformative Friendships: 7 Questions to Deepen Any Relationship* as a tool to help you grow in this area.[2]

- **Someone from each area of life in which sin festered**. This is a direct implication of John's instruction to "walk in the light" during your battle with sin (1 John 1:7). Go back through your full disclosure. Pay attention to the geography. What areas of life (i.e., work, gym, social club, etc.) did your sin begin and grow? Identify a trusted friend who shares, or is willing to honor, your Christian values. Tell them the changes you are making and that you are putting lampposts of accountability and awareness in those areas to dispel the darkness of anonymity or privacy. This can be as simple as, "I want to make a change in my life: [define]. I appreciate our friendship, and you know me well enough in this place to hold me accountable to my commitment."

▶ **Read Hebrews 3:12–15.** The author of Hebrews takes confession very seriously. He takes it seriously because he knows the condition of our hearts when left to their own devices. Do not buy into the lie that you are stronger than Scripture says you are. Unless you take immediate, active steps to begin establishing accountability outside your G4 group, then you are falling into the lie that led you to your sexual sin.

▶ **Read Ecclesiastes 4:9–12.** This is often read as a marriage passage, but it is about friendship in general. Notice two things: First, this passage implies a mutual awareness of our struggles. Everybody in this passage is facing a challenge. Second, notice the number change from two to three. When we obey God by reaching out to other believers in our struggle, God's presence is added to the impact of these relationships to magnify their impact. When we entrust our struggle to a friend through confession, we gain more than the support of that friend. Ecclesiastes 4 teaches us that God is uniquely present in those conversations, strengthening the cords of encouragement and support being built with his presence.

Don't Confess to Your Adultery Partner

If you are married, you should not confess to your adultery partner. Often, we want to do this because we think it will bring closure to a relationship we value. As we said earlier, *closure* is a code word for relapse.

Your act of ending the relationship is a clear indication that you believed the relationship was wrong. Your continued noncommunication with that person is the fruit of repentance that reveals your opinion has not changed. Your silence is an act of protection for both of you. If you speak compassionate words of remorse such as "You're a great person and it tears me up to have to hurt you by ending our relationship," it will only serve to stir up temptation for you both. Trying to make the ending "nice" will reignite a sense that you don't want the relationship to end.

If you were "only" attracted to someone at the level of an emotional affair or other type of forbidden attraction, also do not confess to this person. Confessing this inappropriate attraction with the people listed above is adequate. To confess your romantic feelings to this person may be either socially awkward in a harmful way or a source of intensified temptation.

CONCLUSION

At this point in Step 5, you are merely listing people you should have a longer conversation of confession with. Even with your spouse, this conversation differs from your full disclosure. It will be a conversation about how your sin impacted the other person, rather than a mere acknowledgment of your sin.

We will cover what should and shouldn't be said in those conversations of confession in the remainder of Step 5. At this point, you should be making your list of people you need to talk to and establishing the conviction that you will follow through on those conversations.

G4 GROUP DISCUSSION: STEP 5, PART ONE

As you discuss this material in G4 group, these questions are meant to facilitate a more honest and beneficial dialogue about this material. Anyone is free to respond to whichever questions they choose.

Experienced Members

- What was the most significant, impactful, or difficult conversation of confession that you had?
- What was the greatest point of internal resistance you wrestled with as you worked Step 5?

New Members

- As you think about Step 5, does it distract you from focusing on your current step?
- Who are your key friends outside of G4?
- How can we pray for you?

Everyone

- How do you respond to the statement, "You will only be as free as you are honest. Privacy kills change and fuels sin. Transparency kills sin and fuels change"?

- In what areas of your life do you need a lamppost of accountability?
- Have you experienced a significant setback or victory since last meeting that you should tell the group?

STEP 5

PART TWO

WHAT IS CONFESSION AND HOW DO I COMPLETE IT?

The video for this part of Step 5 can be found at: bradhambrick.com/falselove5p2.

Now we are shifting from who to talk to (Step 5, Part One) to figuring out what to say. Often, confession can be as hard as speaking a second language. If you've ever studied another language, you know the struggle of trying to construct a sentence in the new language. It's normal to have that experience in Step 5 as you transition from speaking in ways that are self-centered, minimizing, and blame-shifting to speaking in ways that are other-minded, responsible, and empathetic.

ACTION STEPS OF CONFESSION

We will navigate the challenges of speaking this new language by identifying seven common ways we can undermine the redemptive power of confession.[1] With each example, we will define key action steps of confession that help ensure confession has the redemptive impact God intends, both in your life and in the lives of those to whom you are confessing.

1. **No friend left behind.** You have already examined the question "Who has been affected by my sin?" (in Step 2 and Step 5, Part One). These are likely people close enough to care about you, and you care about them as well. The general principle is that if someone was impacted by your sin, they should hear your confession.

   Remember, confession is not extreme, and it is not punishment. Those who really want to change involve others. Those who believe their change is good want others to know about that change. Confession is an important transition from a temporary change mindset to a lasting lifestyle of change. When we confess to those affected by our sin, we are transitioning from managing the consequences of our sin to transparent living in pursuit of freedom.

> ▶ **Exercise:** Continue building your list of people you need to confess to because (a) they have been negatively impacted by your sin and (b) they will notice or be affected by the changes you need to make.

2. **No *ifs*, *buts*, or *maybes*.** These are words that radically change the nature of a confession. They mutate confession into blame-shifting or minimization. When you use them, the person you are talking to will likely be concerned that these words show a regression in your journey. If that happens while you are trying to take an important step forward, you may be tempted to be defensive toward their concern. For that reason, we take the time to discuss the impact of these small words.
   - *If* indicates that you doubt the certainty of what you're saying and, therefore, weakens your confession.
   - *But* in the middle of a confession shifts responsibility from what precedes the word *but* to what comes after it.
   - *Maybe* reduces the level of personal commitment to what you are saying and removes confidence from the listener.

   Look at each of these examples, and notice the impact of the three words in question:
   - "*If* I lied to you, I am sorry."
   - "I know it's foolish to seek comfort from pornography, *but* I've done it for so long it's all I know."
   - "*Maybe* I could try to call you when I'm tempted to reach out to my adultery partner."

   This language is very common and represents the kind of tentative phrasing we fall into when we're uncomfortable. But it is also the kind of language that reveals a weak commitment to the change process.

► **Exercise:** As a way of learning to speak without shifting blame or minimizing your struggles, rewrite each of these statements without the troublesome language. Do the same with confession phrases where you commonly use words like *if*, *but*, and *maybe*. Write out the problematic version and then write a version without these terms.

3. **No generic confession.** Confession is more than disclosing a series of wrong actions. It involves revealing who you were and who you are becoming. Secret sin builds a false picture of who you were. Your secrets made everyone around you live in your lie. Confession allows them to live in the truth again or maybe for the first time.

> If someone was impacted by your sin, they should hear your confession.

This raises the question *How specific should I be when confessing sexual sin?* The narrative of David's sin with Bathsheba is instructive for this question. In his repentance to God, David said he would speak of his sin and restoration with others (Psalm 51:13–14). Much of the detail in the biblical account could have only been gleaned from David's confessions. Here we find the items that God divinely inspired to be confessed about David's sexual sin.

► **Read 2 Samuel 11–12.** Below is an outline of this passage. The outline is broken into units to help you use this narrative as a template for thinking through your own confession. You will notice that this passage overlaps significantly with steps you've already completed, and it foreshadows future steps. In this passage, we read David's full journey. It is a fitting time for us to step back from the "trees" of each step and see the "forest" of our full journey. You should confess the following:

11:1—The actions that left you vulnerable to this sin. In David's case, staying home during the war didn't have a sexual connotation, but it did isolate him from his male friends and leave him with an abundance of free time. What choices—whether they have a sexual motivation or not—place you in a vulnerable position for temptation?

11:2–3—The steps that you took to pursue sin. Sin does not "just happen." David took several steps to inquire about, meet, send for, and be alone with Bathsheba. What steps did you take to make your sin possible?

11:4—The full extent of your sin. David was not graphic, but he was clear and did not minimize what he did. Few things are more damaging to any relationship than allowing the severity of sexual sin to slowly leak out. Don't allow a relationship to die the death of a thousand partial confessions.

11:5—All consequences of your sin. David tells us the fallout of his sin. Did you lose your job, get demoted, contract an STD, take out a secret credit card and rack up undisclosed debt, etc.? Unconfessed consequences will be sources of shame and future temptation.

11:6–27—Your methods of deception. Who helped cover up your sin, what other sins did you commit in tandem with the sexual sin, and what impact did the sin have on other areas of your character? Notice this section is the longest part of the narrative. Sin maintains its life and mutates into other expressions when we hide our methods of lying and resist reflecting upon the impact.

12:1–15—How you were brought to repentance. As you confess this, remember that it is God's grace (although painful) that you were brought to repentance. If you were discovered, you can still share how you came to the conviction to be completely truthful and committed to change.

12:7–15—You should accept the consequences that emerge after your confession.

12:16–23—You should willingly walk through the emotional ups and downs of those affected by your sin. Don't vomit your sin on them and walk away, leaving them to clean up the mess alone. Don't demand forgiveness or rush people to trust you. After confession, remain focused on your growth and allow the pace at which other people process the ramifications of your sin in their life to be between them and God.

> ► **Exercise:** Write a 2 Samuel 11–12 version of your story using the outline above. Use this as another way to review your full disclosure to make sure that it is complete, as well as an opportunity to see God's work in your life. Second Samuel 11–12 was painful for David and those who were near him. The things that brought you to G4 were painful. But pain does not mean God is absent or passive.

4. **No self-centered apologies.** Sin has consequences—both intentional and unintentional. Confession expresses empathy and takes responsibility for the dominoes that result from our sin. This is not groveling or penance, both of which are emotionally manipulative. Instead, it is owning the consequences of what we set in motion.

   It is important to remember that the step of confession is not about you. You take this step to care for those you've hurt and deceived. Self-centeredness and selfishness fueled your sin. By contrast, confession is an exercise in other-mindedness. Being unwilling to express remorse for the consequences of our sin reveals the return of the self-centeredness that made our sin seem reasonable.

   Your goal in confession is to represent God more accurately to the person your sin has affected. God is compassionate and understanding to our hurts (Psalm 56:8). Therefore, our confession should include evidence that we have reflected on the impact of our sin on others. It is wise and appropriate to ask the other person how your sin has impacted them. But to ask without taking time to reflect on this personally is lazy and casts doubt on the sincerity of our confession.

   When sharing this aspect of your confession, avoid using verbs of completion (i.e., "I know . . ."). Instead, use process verbs (i.e., those ending in "ing" such as "I am learning . . ."). Avoiding verbs of completion allows the other person to talk about other ways our sin has affected them without it feeling to us like they are piling on.

▶ **Exercise:** Look at the list of people to whom you need to have a confession conversation. Ask yourself how your sin impacted them. What did they think they knew about me that was false? How did I manipulate or mislead them in the pursuit of my sin? What did they not get from me that was reasonable for them to expect? Make this part of your confession.

5. **No plea bargains.** Confession is not a plea bargain or the beginning of a negotiation. Because you see your need to change, your confession should include the following things on the list of potential consequences with people in your life:

    *   I will be transparent about my schedule so that there are fewer times when I feel alone and able to sin.
    *   I will forgo [activity, group, or friendship] because the temptation toward sin is strong there.
    *   I will seek accountability software on my electronic devices to reduce my isolation on these devices.
    *   [Blank] allowed me to lie and cover my activities, so I will [discuss how you will remove that opportunity to deceive].
    *   Any other consequences that are more tailored to your sin.

    Consequences are not punitive. Consequences can play a disciplinary role of reinforcing life lessons and solidifying prevention measures or a trust-building role of providing tangible fruit for an otherwise unverifiable desire to change. Because our Step 5 confession is voluntary, we should view the consequences as trust-building measures.

    Begin by stating the obvious. If there are clear changes you need to make, state them in your confession. Don't phrase them as, "I will do [blank] for you," as if it were a favor or concession, or "If you want me to, I will [blank]," portraying change as punishment. It is more in keeping with confession to say, "Because I see my need to change, I will [blank]."

    End by asking an open-ended question. Honest questions are a sign of humility. They reveal that we are not presenting a contract or deal, but that we are seeking to restore a relationship. A simple question would suffice: "Are there other ways I can show you the sincerity of my desire to change or help you trust me?"

6. **No words—only confessions.** Confession is not the culmination of the journey, as if words alone were sufficient. Confession is merely drawing a map and acknowledging that the journey is needed. Confession involves walking out those actions, not merely verbalizing the map. A lot of energy has been spent to get to this point, and that is why many people stop their travels at the step of confession. But when we stop at confession, our lack of future effort gives the offended person reason to say, "You didn't really mean what you said." This is why our study has four more steps.

> ▶ **Read Luke 14:28–33.** Part of embracing the gospel is counting the cost of following God and embracing the sacrifice. Obviously, it's worth it. We give up our life of sin and its misery in exchange for a life of transformation into what God intended and an eternity in heaven. But it feels painful, and we often want to back out because of our doubt. The same is true with confession because it is rooted in the gospel paradigm of dying to self and living for God's glory through serving others. As you prepare to confess, realize this dynamic is part of the emotional battle.

7. **No entitled or impatient confessions.** "I'm sorry" is not the same thing as asking for forgiveness. "I'm sorry" is an appropriate statement after a mistake. "Will you forgive me?" is the appropriate statement when we have sinned against another person. Be sure you are requesting forgiveness and not merely asking to be excused.

It is also important to remember that while forgiveness is commanded by God, Scripture never calls on the confessing person to remind others of this command. If your sin created mistrust in the other person, then you honor them by being patient. Impatience only exacerbates mistrust.

While Scripture commands others to forgive, it does not appoint you as the timekeeper. Allow at least as much time as it took you to come to repentance. It is hypocritical to expect someone else to process suffering (your sin against them) faster than you acknowledged and committed to change your sin. During the interval between confession and forgiveness, love and serve the other person while continuing to work on your personal change. This helps you remain other-minded, and it honors your friend.

PREPARING FOR A CONFESSING CONVERSATION

Knowing what to say is different from communicating what you intended in the moment of conversation. In the previous section we outlined a conversation. In this section, you will fill in the outline. If we are used to hiding our sexual sin, then speaking with ownership and transparency may feel like speaking in a second language. When we speak in a second language, we take more time to think through and plan what we intend to say. Use the tool at the end of this step to outline the details for the conversations you need to have. Think about the following details as you create the outline:

> Confession is not the culmination of the journey, as if words alone were sufficient. Confession is merely drawing a map and acknowledging that the journey is needed.

- Begin with the list of people you created as you worked through the first point on confession, "No friend left behind." Print one copy of the confession guide for each person on the list (PDF copies are available at bradhambrick.com/falselove).
- The top paragraph is meant to be an overview of the flow of this conversation. It does not need to be spoken but is a map to keep you from getting lost in the details.
- Complete the open-ended statements that follow using your notes from earlier steps.
- If you are concerned about whether you succumb to blame-shifting or self-pity during your confession, rehearse confessing with a pastor, mentor, or counselor.
- Request a time to meet with each person and follow through with your confession.

▶ **Read Philemon.** This short letter tucked in the back of the New Testament is a prepared confession. Paul came to learn of how Onesimus had stolen from Philemon prior to being saved. Onesimus later became a Christian under Paul's teaching. When Onesimus returned to make things right with Philemon, he took along the letter that Paul had written to Philemon. So, in case you are wondering whether this kind of action is necessary or biblical, realize that it was important enough for God to devote a book of the Bible as an example of what you are preparing to do.

G4 GROUP DISCUSSION: STEP 5, PART TWO

As you discuss this material in G4 group, these questions are meant to facilitate a more honest and beneficial dialogue about this material. Anyone is free to respond to whichever questions they choose.

Experienced Members

- What did you learn from your work in Step 5 that you wish you had known before you made your confessions?
- How did allowing time after asking for forgiveness impact those who were hurt most by your addiction?

New Members

- Which of the seven aspects of confession is most unsettling for you?
- What most immediate or obvious consequences of your sexual sin do you need to accept?
- How can we pray for you?

Everyone

- How has the completion of Step 5 felt like speaking in a second language? What are the most valuable things you learned from this exercise?
- How does thinking about the book of Philemon as an illustration of Step 5 impact your reading of it?
- Have you experienced a significant setback or victory since last meeting that you should tell the group?

CONFESSION GUIDE

Name of the person to whom you are confessing: _____

> *"I have not represented God well in your presence [explain]. You have been hurt by my ungodly emotions, attitudes, and actions [describe]. My goal in life is to make God's character known. That starts with this request for forgiveness. I value our relationship more than my pride. I am currently working on submitting my life to God's control, and I understand if you need time to consider my request for forgiveness."*

I am now willing to admit that I sinned against you by . . . [list specific sins and avoid words like *if*, *but*, and *maybe*]. These actions were my choice and were wrong. Review your full disclosure and look for ways this person was impacted by your sin.

I am learning to see how much my life was ruled by the desire for [list motives for your sin]. You did not cause my sin. Refer to the relevant motives from Step 3.

I am beginning to see how my sin has affected you [describe]. Has my sin impacted your life in ways that I have not yet seen? Refer to relevant responses in your Step 2 work on the impact of your sin on others and your notes on "No Self-Centered Apologies" in Step 5.

I know I must change to honor God and to bless those I care about. Because I see my need for change, I will [list obvious needed changes]. I am still learning what other changes honoring God will require of me. State those changes that are foundational.

Are there other ways I can show you the sincerity of my desire to change or help you trust me in the areas where I've brought unhealthiness into our relationship? [Pause and take notes on their answer.] This section should be blank until you speak with the person.

I understand if it will take some time, but I am asking for your forgiveness. Thank you for showing me the honor of listening.

STEP 5
PART THREE

GUIDANCE FOR MAKING AMENDS

The video for this part of Step 5 can be found at: bradhambrick.com/falselove5p3.

S o far we have learned how to take ownership of our sin, the need to see how our sin impacted others, and how to have a confessional conversation without blame-shifting, minimizing, or falling into self-pity. Now we will look at the final part of this step—seeking to restore what we can of what our sin destroyed.

In the 12-Step group model of AA, SA, etc., Step 8 asks you to make a list of all persons harmed by your actions and be willing to make amends to each of them. Then Step 9 asks you to make amends wherever possible, except when doing so would injure them or others. Step 5 of this G4 curriculum combines these tasks.

Remember, making amends is meant to be restorative, not cathartic; you are not trying to get something off you (relief) but to make something more whole for others (repair). This brings us back to the exception given by AA. Sometimes seeking to make amends can be harmful to the other person. If you have doubt about whether your confession would be more harmful than helpful, seek the guidance of a pastor, friend, or counselor.

However, for most situations, the Bible encourages making amends. Restitution is required for the thief (in Exodus 22:1) and prescribed for the person who remembers his brother has something against him while offering a sacrifice (in Matthew 5:22–23). Making amends is the action of sincerity. And it is the action that can lead to restored relationships.

FOUR TYPES OF AMENDS

As you think about making amends, it can sometimes be difficult to discern what to do about things that happened in the past or if the effects were less tangible. For that reason, we will consider direct amends, narrative amends, living amends, and symbolic amends.

> Making amends is meant to be restorative, not cathartic; you are not trying to get something off you (relief) but to make something more whole for others (repair).

Direct Amends

Direct amends are repayment for tangible and measurable offenses. These are the clearest form of amends. As you make direct amends, you are facing the history of your sin in a new way. You are experiencing the impact your sin had on others. This experience should further remove any remaining tendency toward minimizing your sin.

- Example: Replacing the office computer that was incapacitated by a virus from a pornography website.
- Example: Returning money recorded as business expenses that you used for lunch dates with your adultery partner.

▶ **Reflection:** What *direct amends* do you need to make and to whom?

Narrative Amends

Narrative amends are required for offenses that result in damage in the form of mistrust or confusion. Now you are looking at the damage done via lies rather than finances or recklessness. To the degree that your sin was motivated by escaping pain, this form of amends requires growing in maturity by facing the pain we caused. This experience should further remove the self-centered form of thinking that often emerges from habituated sin.

- Example: Clarify with mutual friends misrepresentations and slander about your spouse that you used to justify your sin.
- Example: Take responsibility for your sin so that others will not be laden with false guilt.

► **Reflection:** What *narrative amends* do you need to make and to whom?

Living Amends

Living amends are for offenses that can only be relieved by a commitment to healthy relating. Now you are looking at the damage done to hearts and relationships, rather than bank accounts and property. If you have not realized it before, people love you and are affected by your self-destructive choices. This experience should reinforce the importance of completing this journey. You are giving people who love you hope. Your continued growth protects that hope.

- Example: Committing to authenticity with your spouse, children, friends, or family members you closed out while you were devoted to your sin.
- Example: Committing to a process of handling insecurity or failure differently so that those who love you don't fear these will take you back into a sinful lifestyle.

► **Reflection:** What *living amends* do you need to make and to whom?

Symbolic Amends

Symbolic amends are for offenses that are highly inaccessible but result in significant emotional disruption. These amends will likely be responses to the parts of your sin that haunt you most. Admittedly, symbolic amends rarely provide as much closure as we would like. This experience helps us quit running from things we can't change. By way of medical metaphor, these amends are for deep cuts. Embracing God's forgiveness makes them nonlethal. Making symbolic amends removes the infection, but scars may remain. We can allow those scars to remind us of the preciousness and frailty of life. We can also use those scars as tools to warn and teach others.

- Example: If you were estranged from your children because of your sin, you might spend extra time encouraging new G4 participants who are estranged from their family because of their sin.

- Example: If your sexual sin resulted in pregnancy and you chose or pressured your partner to choose an abortion, you might volunteer or donate to a crisis pregnancy center.

▶ **Reflection:** What *symbolic amends* do you need to make and to whom?

THE IMPACT OF MAKING AMENDS

This step can be one of the more emotionally painful steps to take. Looking into the eyes of those you've hurt and hearing their experience—even hearing their forgiveness—can be very emotionally straining. That is why it is important to have a group, mentor, pastor, or counselor guide you in this step.

Be patient with the process. When something is painful, our tendency is usually to either quit or speed through it. But both are counterproductive responses. One of your goals in this step is to engage your G4 journey with sober-mindedness—that is, with the mentality and life habits of someone committed to an accurate view of life.

As we conclude the instructional part of this step and you begin enacting it, it is good to remember the purpose of Step 5. We are prone to view this step as penance—a form of punishing ourselves for being bad so that we'll be less likely to be bad again in the future. This is *not* the purpose of confessing and making amends. We confess and make amends to terminate the lifestyle of living as if nothing happened and imposing that lifestyle on those who love us. We acknowledge past sin and seek to mend its impact so that we, and those around us, can live cohesive lives instead of lives segmented by a collection of off-limit subjects and false assumptions.

This is the step when you realize that **John 8:32** is not an individualized truth. "You will know the truth, and the truth will set you free" when you are not in control of the "truth" everyone has access to, but when you allow yourself and those around you to live freely without secrets, guilt, or shame.

▶ **Read Luke 19:1–10.** Notice that when Zacchaeus is convicted of a lifestyle of stealing and deceit, his first instinct is to make amends (v. 8). Don't get distracted by the numbers (i.e., half and fourfold). That would be using Zacchaeus's testimony as a prescription or recipe. Instead, notice that Jesus affirms this response in Zacchaeus (v. 9). It is not that making amends saved Zacchaeus, but the willingness to make amends was an expression of bearing fruit in keeping with repentance (Luke 3:8). As you complete Step 5, you are also bearing fruit that validates what God has been doing in your heart throughout this journey.

G4 GROUP DISCUSSION: STEP 5, PART THREE

As you discuss this material in G4 group, these questions are meant to facilitate a more honest and beneficial dialogue about this material. Anyone is free to respond to whichever questions they choose.

Experienced Members

- What was the most difficult amends that you needed to make?
- What was the most impactful amends you made and how did it impact you?

New Members

- Are you prone to feel rushed and intimidated by this Step? Be honest about that.
- Are you encouraged by the possibility of living a "less haunted" life?
- How can we pray for you?

Everyone

- Have you realized you need to make amends that you have not made yet?
- In your own words, describe the difference between penance (what Step 5 is not) and refusing to live as if the past didn't happen (what Step 5 is).
- Have you experienced a significant setback or victory since last meeting that you should tell the group?

STEP 6
RESTRUCTURE MY LIFE
to rely on God's grace and Word
to transform my life.

At the end of this step, I want to be able to say . . .

"To this point in my G4 journey, I have learned
a great deal about myself [list with examples],
my sin [examples], and my Savior [list with
examples]. Because of these truths, I want and need
to make the following changes [list]. My temptation
is to see these changes as a way to become
independent from God and others, rather than
cooperating with and celebrating God's grace
in my life with others on the same kind of journey."

STEP 6
PART ONE

LIVING WITH LIMITS

The video for this part of Step 6 can be found at: bradhambrick.com/falselove6p1.

This is probably the step you were looking for when you started this journey. We intuitively want practical tips and strategies for change. These things are helpful and good. But they require a solid foundation to be effective. For five steps you have been laying that foundation of honesty, commitment, and garnering social support.

Now that you've laid this foundation, the strategies we'll discuss in Step 6 can be effective. You are no longer minimizing your struggle. You are being honest about your history. You have begun facing difficult emotions like shame, regret, and guilt, instead of escaping them. You have people supporting you. With these things in place, the approaches we will discuss don't have to magically make your sin go away. They can merely support and reinforce the honest life of integrity you're already living.

We will look at four strategy clusters for restructuring your life to rely on God's grace and Word. Select the approaches that fit your struggle best. Don't feel compelled to try to incorporate everything we cover. We will consider living with limits, embracing self-control, restoring honor in relationships, and strengthening your soul.

As you prepare to work through this step, here are three principles to keep in mind:

1. **Change is not as complicated as dysfunction.** In Step 6, don't expect to read something profound. Lies are complicated; honesty is simple. Integrity is a much simpler way to live than hiding sexual

sin. Because of this, we can be encouraged that these strategies don't have to be complex to be effective.

2. **You have more influence over your sin than anyone or anything else.** We have emphasized the truth that we are powerless without Christ (John 15:5). We will now begin to emphasize the complementing (not contradicting) truth that God intends to deliver you in your day-to-day, seemingly inconsequential choices.

3. **Change plans must be (a) acceptable—something you voluntarily embrace, (b) accessible—feasible for your circumstances, and (c) effective—well-suited for your struggle.** As you select from the buffet of strategies below, allow these criteria to help you select the best-fit options for you.

LIVING WITH LIMITS

To understand the importance of living with limits, let's create a metaphor. When the chief technology designer in a computer company uses their laptop, that computer does not just obey the designer's prompts because he bought it. The computer obeys its designer at a much deeper level because he invented it. If the computer tried to function outside of its design, it would break. This metaphor, while silly in its personification of a laptop, helps us see something important.

God is our creator who also purchased us by the blood of Jesus (1 Corinthians 6:19–20). At this point in our journey, we need to realize that we don't obey God only because he bought us, but because he designed us and we break when we try to function in ways that are at odds with his design. Like all metaphors, this one eventually breaks down. Unlike computers, we obey God because we choose to and because we love him. For all these reasons, this part of Step 6 will explore three areas of limitation that we need to live within to honor God's design: (1) physical, (2) emotional, and (3) logistical.

Living Within Our Physical Limits

Neglecting our body pushes our physical limits and lets our soul suffer. When we fail to honor our physical limitations, we increase the number and intensity of temptations we face. We also decrease our resolve and resiliency to face those temptations. Ask yourself these questions to look at various realms of caring for your physical body:

- Sleep—Am I getting six to eight hours of sleep per night? ___ Yes ___ No
- Diet—Am I eating regular, healthy, balanced meals? ___ Yes ___ No
- Exercise—Am I strengthening and maintaining my body? ___ Yes ___ No
- Time management—Am I living productive but not overly filled days? ___ Yes ___ No
- Substances—Am I abstaining from alcohol or drugs that lower my inhibitions? ___ Yes ___ No

The more often you marked *no*, the more difficult it will be to pursue sexual integrity, but there is good news! These are choices you can make. Go to bed at a decent hour. Put more green stuff in your diet. Go for a walk. Review your schedule and simplify it. The less time and money you invest in your sin, the more time and money you will have to invest in these replenishing outlets. For five steps you have been carving out the time and money you need to reinvest in God-honoring pursuits.

▶ **Read Mark 14:38 and 1 Timothy 4:7–10.** When we care well for our body, it is a friend of our soul. When we neglect our body, it becomes an obstacle to the soul. In Mark 14, Jesus prayed for his disciples because their flesh was weak: The long day of traveling, followed by a big Passover meal with lots of wine, would have made them weary as they tried to pray late at night in a quiet garden. Paul tells Timothy there is a connection between bodily training and spiritual training—that is, discipline in one area of life makes self-control easier to express in other areas of life. Will an exercise routine, healthy diet, and regular sleep schedule remove temptation from your life? No. Will the absence of these things increase temptation in your life? Yes.

▶ **Reflection:** What changes do you need to make to take better care of your physical limits?

Living Within Our Emotional Limits

It is important not to feel condemned for natural attractions and arousal. It is not wrong to experience attraction or be aroused. It is wrong to lust. If we are going to be emotionally fair with ourselves, we need to understand the difference. Lust is entertaining ourselves with attraction and arousal. Attraction is noticing; lust is fixating. Arousal is a physical response; lust is wrapping an illicit narrative around that physical response.

Living within our emotional limits requires us to **redefine *reward*** and similar words. As sin becomes ingrained in our lives, it becomes our reward of choice. When sin is our reward, doing something well becomes a moment of temptation. We begin to feel cheated if we don't get to engage in sexual sin. God is perceived as a prude and cosmic killjoy. How we define *reward* has a myriad of emotional implications.

▶ **Read Psalm 84:7–12.** When sin is our reward of choice, it is hard to believe that "No good thing does he [God] withhold from those who walk uprightly" (v. 11). Sin makes righteous living feel like a burden that saps our strength, rather than a well of life that takes us from "strength to strength" (v. 7). A primary part of change is gaining a definition of good that agrees with God's definition of good.

▶ **Reflection:** How can you reward yourself in wholesome ways when you've done something well? How would having a list of God-honoring ways to reward yourself help you live within your emotional limits?

Living within our emotional limits requires us to realize that it is **easier to resist temptation than to resist sin we've already entered into**. While it is true that temptation is not sin, it is equally true that flirting with temptation is foolish. We cannot run on the wet, thin ice of temptation and expect not to fall into the pond of sin. Let us not deceive ourselves into thinking that we can be reckless, foolish saints for long.

▶ **Reflection:** What compromising situations make your sin feel irresistible? What steps do you take to put yourself in these moments? What would it look like to fight sin earlier in the temptation cycle?

Living within our emotional limits requires us to recognize that sexual sin is a powerful multisensory escape. Sexual sin involves sight, touch, sounds, and imagination. Sexual sin simultaneously captivates multiple regions of the brain. This is why sexual sin effectively distracts us from unpleasant emotions. For this reason, pursuing sexual integrity will require us to mature in how we process sadness, disappointment, failure, stress, and other unpleasant emotions.

> ▶ **Reflection:** What unpleasant emotions do you need to learn to process better for the multisensory escape of sexual sin to be less powerful? What would emotional maturity look like in those unpleasant moments?

Living Within Our Logistical Limits

By the time a particular sin has become life dominating, it has made itself at home in our life. We often don't notice the dozens of ways we tailor our life to make it easier to sin. For this reason, pursuing sexual integrity entails rearranging parts of our lives. A life of sexual integrity will be different than merely your current life minus sexual sin. It will be a life minus all the accommodations your sin requires.

Think about the changes you could implement. The suggestions below are not meant to be exhaustive; rather, they are meant to spark your thinking. However, if any item on the list would help you resist sexual sin, please voluntarily embrace it. You have not come this far on your journey to begin doing things "good enough" now. Would it help you in your journey to add any of the following to your routines?

- *Internet filter*: This is also known as blocking software. Its purpose is to prevent a computer from being able to access sexual websites. Filters are never sufficient by themselves. You can get around them if you want to. But they can be beneficial speed bumps in moments of temptation.
- *Accountability software*: These types of programs send email reports to a designated accountability partner when a questionable site is visited or if the program is turned off while the

computer is running. In this way, you are never "alone" with your computer. While there are many versions of this software available, we recommend Covenant Eyes as a quality option.

- *Access internet in public settings*: This might mean moving your computer to a high-traffic area of your home, going to bed at the same time as your spouse, working from a coffee shop, or other comparable changes. Might these be inconvenient changes? Yes. But the main point is that no convenience is worth compromising your character or hurting your family.

- *Put Scripture near where you experience temptation*: Where there is darkness put light. Review your full disclosure. List the places you referenced. Review your Step 3 motives–triggers. Identify passages of Scripture that counter these points of deception. The most effective passages of Scripture may have little to do with lust. At this stage in your journey, use the Bible to point you toward hope and light more than away from darkness and sin.

> No convenience is worth compromising your character or hurting your family.

- *Don't gaze at what is not yours*: Think of lust as sexual stealing. You are taking what has not been covenanted to you. You are forcing someone to do in your imagination what they would not do voluntarily.

> If you are a man, start viewing women as your sisters, as people to protect instead of prey upon. If you are a woman, start treating men as your brothers rather than turning them into romantic-erotic objects. . . . If you are married, begin the hard work of building an honest relationship where sexuality becomes one of the fruits of your unity as a couple.
> —David Powlison[1]

- *Don't visit suggestive stores or sites*: Enough temptation will find you. Don't make Satan's hunt easier. Relying on hedges of protection as your solution for lust is legalism. However, not having these protections in place is foolishness.

- *Do activities you enjoy*: You are not merely trying to extricate lust from life. You are discovering the life that God intended for you to enjoy. If overcoming lust is only about what you don't do, you will begin to feel strongly discouraged. As your desires are purified, you should find things you enjoy doing within God's positive gifts.

  ▶ **Reflection:** What logistical changes do you need to make in your life? If you were serious about pursuing sexual integrity, what changes would you have already made?

CONCLUSION

Limits are our friends. Limits are good. A life without limits is bad and dangerous. Those are simple, but profound sentences. When embraced, these truths start to change our life for the better. When embraced, limits are the key to experiencing true freedom. As you do the work of Step 6, ask yourself whether you believe that.

> When embraced, limits are the key to experiencing true freedom.

At this point in your journey, you should be settling into the answer yes, wise limits are positive in your life. Don't rush past that profound change. It is a monumental shift, much like the person working out shifts from disliking sore muscles to appreciating that sore muscles are a sign of growing strength. It is a sign that your core values are changing.

G4 GROUP DISCUSSION: STEP 6, PART ONE

As you discuss this material in G4 group, these questions are meant to facilitate a more honest and beneficial dialogue about this material. Anyone is free to respond to whichever questions they choose.

Experienced Members

- What limit were you most resistant to accepting? What difference did it make when you relented?
- What logistical change made the biggest difference in your pursuit of sexual integrity?

New Members

- What simple change do you need to make this week?
- What is your reaction to the statement "Change is not as complicated as dysfunction"?
- How can we pray for you?

Everyone

- What is your honest response to the devotional on Psalm 84?
- What unpleasant emotion do you need to better learn to maturely process?
- Have you experienced a significant setback or victory since last meeting that you should tell the group?

STEP 6
PART TWO

EMBRACING SELF-CONTROL

The video for this part of Step 6 can be found at: bradhambrick.com/falselove6p2.

We cannot root out sin like children cleaning their rooms—piling everything in the closet or under the bed. Long periods of neglect with bursts of quick-fix activity won't get the job done. Why not? Sin is part lion and part rabbit—it hunts and it multiplies. Unless we methodically eradicate sin, it will overtake our life as we hide, ignore, or minimize it.

Notice that this applies to more than sexual sin. Any neglected sin is a gateway sin. When we give way to indiscretion in one area of life, the disruption and temptation that ensues becomes a foothold for the reemergence of sexual sin. Think back to Step 3. How many roles did sexual sin play in your life? This means that sexual sin is a primary temptation you're likely to face when lack of self-control creates disruption in your life.

We are not saying that organized people are holy and unorganized people are unholy. Holiness is not easier to achieve for type A people. The point is that the gravity of sin works against our pursuit of holiness, so we must be intentional if we are going to grow in our ability to love God and love others.

FOUR AREAS OF SELF-CONTROL

As we consider self-control, we will delve into four areas to evaluate and monitor. These are money, schedule, authority, and pleasure/desire.

Money

Financial habits and sexual sin are often intertwined. The following four connections are a starting point:

1. Pornography is an industry that strives to make money. It's very good at making money. Even if you're not paying for subscriptions to pornography sites, the frequency of your clicks is funding the industry.
2. Spending that is unaccounted for feeds the lie, "I can get away with this. No one will know."
3. Spending that is unaccounted for feeds the lie, "This is my money, and I should be able to do with it what I want."
4. Adultery costs money. Secrets, including hidden spending, create distance from your spouse and make it easier to be close to someone who should be an outsider to your marriage.

Having disciplined and (if married) transparent financial management requires something unpopular—sacrifice. When decisions are made jointly, you run the risk of not getting what you want. You might have to say no to self to say yes to your marriage or God. This is the essence of sexual sin's appeal—never having to say no to self because another person or God disapproves.

The more money you've spent in pursuit of your sexual sin, the more important it is for you to have a budget and track your spending. Having a budget and tracking your spending is a basic principle of wise living. That is why, even if you did not spend money on your sexual sin, tracking your spending is an important part of investing your life in things that matter and give life.

▶ **Reflection:** Does your current financial management provide consistent (weekly or monthly) awareness of how you are investing your life? Does your current financial management process compel you to invest your life—both money and time—in things that are meaningful and wholesome?

▶ **Read Matthew 6:21.** Perhaps you remember the transitive principle from algebra class. It said, "If A equals B and B equals C, then A equals C." We can use a version of that principle to apply this passage in Matthew. If your heart is where your treasure is, then your heart will follow where you invest your treasure. When we are pursuing a changed heart, we can and should leverage this principle to our advantage. Stewarding our money wisely and transparently helps us to tame the lustful desires of our heart. As you change your spending habits to become more intentional, godly, and transparent, your heart will conform to (i.e., begin to follow) the lifestyle you are investing in. Don't be flippant with your money because being financially diligent will make it harder for you to be careless with your heart.

Schedule

Think back to Step 6, Part One and the number of hours you devoted to your sin. Those are blocks of hours during your week. If you are going to reclaim those hours, you need to express more self-control over your schedule. It is not just that you have spent many hours doing wrong things, but also you need to find different, God-honoring ways to invest those hours. Instead, those hours should be filled with the following:

- productive, meaningful activities
- enjoyable, satisfying activities
- loving activities that honor significant people in your life
- healthy, restful activities to care for your body
- devotional activities that would enrich your relationship with him

In a schedule lacking self-control, a schedule with large blocks of time given to sexual sin, we don't feel like we have time for any of these activities. We feel like God and other people are demanding too much. So what do we do? We retreat to sexual sin and waste more time that robs us of the good things God wants for us.

▶ **Reflection:** Go back to your full disclosure. Think of your full disclosure as a schedule rather than a confession. If you were your own time manager, what would you change? What would you devote the wasted blocks of time to? How do you begin to get excited about the new possibilities that emerge?

Whatever changes you are excited about—and yes, by now change should be exciting—share them with a few friends. Don't tell only people in G4 about these desired changes. Start talking about these changes in your larger social support network.

Make a plan that allows you to begin implementing those changes. Changes in your schedule are changes in habits. Habits in our life are deeply ingrained through repetition—like our schedule—and don't change without a high degree of intentionality. Rethinking your schedule is an excellent way to see what your life could be like without the sponge of sexual sin absorbing your hours.

> ▶ **Reflection:** What are your favorite wholesome pleasures? Maybe they include spending time outdoors, a hobby, sports, good food, fancy coffee, or something else. Are those things in your new schedule? Be sure to add new activities.

It is not selfish to regularly schedule things you enjoy. Selflessness isn't boring and drab. God is not against your pleasure. God is against your sin. God is against your sin because he is for you and those you care about.

> ▶ **Read Ephesians 5:15–17.** Notice that this passage says "the days are evil." In context, Paul is not talking about the end times or the tribulation. Paul is talking about living unintentional lives. He is calling on these believers to examine their lives and look at how they're living. When he says, "the days are evil," he is observing what happens when we live without a plan. In effect, Paul is saying a God-honoring, satisfying life won't happen by accident. Mindless people drift toward sin and folly. Sin and folly produce angst and regret, not enduring satisfaction. Paul is saying, "Be intentional about filling your schedule with good, satisfying, worthwhile activities. Otherwise, life will get worse, not better."

Authority

Sexual sin, like all sin, requires a strong distaste for the word *no*. We like the idea of being free from sin, but we dislike the idea of having our options limited. Rationally, we can acknowledge that these are two sides of the same coin. Emotionally, it is amazing how quickly a limit on our freedom—even for something we want to be free from—can make us sour toward anyone (God, accountability partner, G4 group, spouse, etc.) or anything (the Bible, the church, moral standards, etc.) that gets in the way of what we want.

God is not against your pleasure. God is against your sin because he is for you and those you care about.

When we become a Christian, we submitted to God's right as Creator to define right and wrong. If we are married, we agreed to honor our spouse with our eyes, affections, and actions. When we committed to a G4 group or an accountability relationship, we chose the area(s) of our life we wanted to change. Each of these are voluntary relationships. It is hypocritical for us to be upset with the limits that emerge from relationships we voluntarily initiated.

▶ **Reflection:** When and how are you prone to get upset with God or people playing a role you invited them to play? When and how are you prone to resent basic standards of sexual integrity? When you resist these standards, how do you misrepresent the people who call you to honor these standards?

▶ **Read Galatians 3:23–29.** Notice that the standard of Scripture is said to feel like bondage before we became Christians (v. 23). The Bible is honest about internal resistance we innately feel toward its moral standards. After coming to Christ, we view what once felt like bondage as protection (v. 24). All the cultural, religious, and gender differences that we might have blamed our internal resistance on are only distractions (v. 28). After we embrace the gospel by faith (vv. 24–26), we view the standards of Scripture as freedom—that is, as the essence of a satisfying life that provides pleasure without the aftertaste of guilt, regret, shame, pain, and relational turmoil. We realize God was exercising his authority over our life, not to constrict our life satisfaction, but to maximize and preserve it.

Pleasure/Desire

What wholesome pleasures has sexual sin crowded out of your life? Whether or not you consider your struggle to pursue sexual integrity an addiction, hear the words of Mark Laaser as if they are spoken to you.

> Recovering sex addicts also need to learn how to play. . . . Recovery is not all pain and blackness. It is about enjoying life and the world God has given. . . . This may sound a bit trite, but addicts are searching for joy and spontaneity and sometimes a toy can help them rediscover these things. —Mark Laaser[1]

By "toy" he simply means something fun and enjoyable. Hiking outdoors, reading a good book, cooking, sewing, playing a favorite sport, spending time with friends, planning a trip, writing music, shopping, tracing your family tree, playing board games, exercising, etc. Engaging these wholesome pleasures is a pivotal part of reclaiming the time surrendered to sexual sin.

> ► **Exercise:** What wholesome pleasure(s) do you want to begin regularly incorporating into your life? Create a list for them.

BUT THIS IS STILL DIFFICULT

Yes, this journey is still difficult. A good plan doesn't make a hard journey easy. As we strive to increase the amount of self-control we express in our life, we experience challenges in new ways. Unless we talk about these challenges, we can become unduly discouraged. Below are two ways to combat the discouragement that comes when we struggle to express self-control.

Look Beyond the Moment

Self-control requires a long-game mentality. But too often we think of "long game" as code for "never." Self-control doesn't mean never enjoying life; it means we enjoy life in ways that last. It means refusing to accept short-term pleasures that create long-term pain. Think of it like a wise investment plan. Investing (a term of financial self-control) doesn't mean never spending money. Instead, it means choosing to save for the down payment on a home rather than going out to eat three times per week.

How does someone embrace this kind of self-control? They learn to look beyond the moment. When they crave going out for fajitas, they remind themselves they want to be a homeowner more than they want the convenience of not cooking and doing dishes. Pursuing the more valuable thing helps them forego the lesser thing.

> ▶ **Reflection:** Write out the long-game benefits of being a person of integrity. Put it in your own language. As you make your list, recite each item using this fill-in-the-blank exercise:

> Because I want [more important thing] I am choosing to forgo sexual sin.

> It is worth the time to write this sentence for each item on your list.

> ▶ **Summary Exercise:** Once you have that list of sentences, write a description of the person you will become as you live out these values.

> ▶ **Example of a Summary Exercise:** I'm tired of feeling guilty and regretting the things I didn't do because I wasted time sinning. I want to be the kind of person who invests my time in the things that are important to me. I want the freedom that comes from being able to look my spouse and friends in the eye without feeling like I'm hiding something. I want to be able to pursue roles of service and leadership in my church without feeling like a hypocrite. I want to be able to receive a compliment from my spouse or friends and simply respond, "Thank you," instead of being haunted by self-talk replying "They wouldn't say that if they knew." I want the emotional and mental freedom of a clean conscience.

Consider a Sexual Fast

If abstaining from sexual sin results in withdrawal symptoms, that indicates your struggle with sexual sin has been at an addictive level. Symptoms of withdrawal include being apathetic, distracted, or easily agitated or experiencing mood swings, sleep disruption, etc. Too often, we vilify our spouse for punishing us when we experience the withdrawal symptoms of our excessive sexual activity. That is blame-shifting and wrong. If your sexual sin has reached an addictive level, a sexual fast may be an important step for you to take even if you are married.

This type of fast would involve no sexual intercourse, no masturbation, and only mild affection (simple kisses or hugs) for a designated period of time. Your spouse should be told of the fast and the rationale for it. This fast is not a form of self-punishment. Instead, the fast is a way to prove to yourself that sex is not ultimate and that real, vulnerable relationships are worth maintaining, even without sex. This fast should be long enough to reinforce

> Self-control is a greater and truer freedom than the permission to do whatever I want.

this point. Often couples will choose between two and three months. During this time your focus is not primarily on abstinence, but on honoring and enjoying God and one another. You are acclimating to the reality that sex is a blessing, not a necessity.

Why would a couple choose to do this? Because it does not honor your spouse to place addictive-level sexual expectations on your marital intimacy. Marital sex is not the cure for sexual addiction. If sex is viewed as ultimate, it will never be satisfying or serve the function it was intended to have within marriage.

CONCLUSION

We can summarize this part of Step 6 with the following sentence: Self-control is a greater and truer freedom than the permission to do whatever I want. That may sound counterintuitive. From the time we were young, most of us defined freedom as the ability to do what we want.

We're not changing our first definition; we're merely nuancing it. The ability to do what we want implies the ability to restrain ourselves from doing what we don't want to do. The potty-trained toddler is freer than the toddler who is not. While the untrained toddler goes to the bathroom whenever and wherever they want, we can easily see that this is not true freedom. Self-control provides a better life.

Anyone who has tried to potty train a child knows the child will disbelieve this seemingly irrefutable truth. The child is deeply offended at the parents' attempt to control them. There is a good chance that if we had used this illustration back at Step 1, we would have been equally offended by it. But the fact that you can hear this illustration with a sheepish smile is a sign of how much God has grown you on this journey. Be encouraged.

G4 GROUP DISCUSSION: STEP 6, PART TWO

As you discuss this material in G4 group, these questions are meant to facilitate a more honest and beneficial dialogue about this material. Anyone is free to respond to whichever questions they choose.

Experienced Members

- How has your attitude toward authority figures in your life changed during your G4 journey?
- Was a 90-day sexual fast part of your journey and, if so, how did you benefit from it?

New Members

- What wholesome pleasures would you have more time to engage by forgoing your sexual sin?
- Are you making any current financial expenditures related to your sexual sin?
- How can we pray for you?

Everyone

- Where do you need to add discipline or be honest about needed changes to your schedule?
- What is your response to these statements: Selflessness isn't boring and drab. God is not against your pleasure. God is against your sin. God is against your sin because he is for you and those you care about.
- Have you experienced a significant setback or victory since last meeting that you should tell the group?

STEP 6
PART THREE

RESTORING HONOR IN RELATIONSHIPS

The video for this part of Step 6 can be found at: bradhambrick.com/falselove6p3.

Pursuing sexual integrity will change all your relationships, not just your romantic relationships. In Part Three of Step 6, we will define what it means to put honor at the forefront of how you relate to people. We need to realize that honoring others is foundational to all relationships that are mutually life-giving.

When honor is central to our relationships, we can begin to experience a deeper level of vulnerability and trust than we've known before. That may sound both intimidating and appealing, but it's worth it and necessary to solidify the change you've been cultivating in this G4 journey. We'll do this by exploring the following three topics:

1. Removing relational patterns of dishonor
2. Cultivating relational patterns of honor
3. Restoring honor in marriage

SEVEN WAYS TO REMOVE RELATIONAL PATTERNS OF DISHONOR

Relational patterns can promote dishonor in two ways: They can either *feed* our sin, or they can *hide* our sin. By the time we arrive at Step 6, we want to do more than merely avoid porn, masturbation, an emotional affair partner, or sex outside of marriage. All these actions express dishonor toward others, but merely removing these actions is not enough. We also want to begin eradicating dishonor at a more fundamental level.

1. **Don't participate in crude humor.** We return to the theme that lust is not just visual. It includes any use of sex for dishonorable

entertainment. What is the implication? Refrain from sexualized humor. When you joke about sex in unwholesome ways, you are portraying lust to yourself and others as lighthearted, insignificant, and amusing. You begin to blur the line between wholesome sexuality and lust with the pleasant vehicle of laughter.

▶ **Read Ephesians 5:3–8.** If you are given to crude, sexualized humor, then this is another passage you should memorize. Notice that Paul connects crude joking (v. 4) with allowing ourselves to be deceived (v. 6). Humor is powerfully convincing. This is why many of the most successful commercials are funny. When we laugh at something, we deem it desirable. When we laugh at lust, we are lowering our guard to something Satan intends to ensnare us.

▶ **Reflection:** When and with whom are you most prone to participate in crude humor? How have you seen these times lower your resolve to pursue sexual integrity?

2. **Don't play the "six degrees of separation" conversation game.** When we are living in sin, we do not want to talk about our sin or anything connected to our sin—or anything connected to anything connected to our sin. To hide, we want more and more separation between us and any subject even tangentially related to our sin. The result is that the good influences in our life become increasingly superficial. That is our fault. Whenever you find yourself avoiding a subject because it is related to something you want to hide, you should consider this a *huge red flag*! At that moment, you should speak to someone in your support network, even if the subject doesn't seem immediately relevant to your G4 journey. This will help to prevent the habit of living in secrecy from reemerging.

▶ **Reflection:** When have you recently caught yourself playing the "six degrees of separation" conversation game? What subjects do you avoid? With whom do you avoid them?

3. **Don't feed the gender stereotype storylines.** We live in a culture where gender stereotypes are overly shaped by the narratives

of the lust industry—pornography for men and romances for women. Neither talks about real people in real relationships sharing real life with real limits and real stressors. Both feed an unrealistic or exaggerated style of relationship centered upon our greatest desires. The more we engage these storylines, the harder it is to experience other-minded, servant-oriented contentment in relationships.

> ▶ **Reflection:** What gender stereotype storylines most feed your struggle with lust, and what promotes them? In what seemingly innocent ways do you feed these storylines?

4. **Don't express hurt with the secondary emotions of anger or self-pity.** Secondary emotions are how we feel about our primary emotions. If our primary emotion is embarrassment over our sin, our secondary emotion might be anger at the person who discovered our sin or self-pity about the consequences of our sin being known. The more we express our hurt with secondary emotions, the less authentic our relationships will be.[1] One man gives this testimony:

> It means trusting my welfare to God when my wife doesn't do what I want. . . . I've become less angry. I don't withdraw into self-pity and lick my wounds. . . . Not falling into self-pity has been one more nail that keeps that door shut tight. I think I've become more honest and constructive, instead of either avoiding my wife or attacking her. —Testimony in David Powlison's *Pornography: Slaying the Dragon*[2]

When you use secondary emotions, you become convinced that no one really understands you. As this belief becomes solidified, because you only expressed secondary emotions, it becomes easier and more "logical" to escape into a fantasy relationship with porn, which has the advantage of being a story in your mind and therefore automatically "understands" you. Or you escape to an adultery partner / emotional affair, who only needs to hear you complain and agree with what you say to seem understanding.

▶ **Reflection:** What primary, more vulnerable, emotions do you tend to avoid? What secondary emotions, such as aggression or defensiveness, do you rely on most? With whom does this problematic tendency occur?

5. **Don't flirt.** Flirting is any behavior that creates or seeks to create romantic interest, sexual tension, an emotional high, or an exclusive bond. These things are not inherently bad, but unless they are part of a committed and wholesome relationship, they can be significant points of temptation. As you pursue sexual integrity, be mindful about doing these things in mix-gendered settings where calling attention to yourself would be wrong.

- *Inside jokes*: Inside jokes and innuendos that others don't understand contribute to an exclusive dynamic—that is, a sense that you and the other person share something unique and special. Everyone else is on the outside and your bond grows because you share something that only the two of you understand.
- *Mimicking*: When we mimic a non-offensive behavior, it communicates "I am paying attention to you," or "I remember how you do things," or "What you do stands out to me." The more we communicate that we are paying attention to the details of their life and mannerisms, the more we're communicating a desire for a deeper relationship.
- *Choices to match known preferences*: Changing your day-to-day choices indicates more than a passing thought about someone. It is a warning signal if you change what you wear, your cologne/perfume, your routine to ensure the two of you are at the same place at the same time, etc. to match the preference of someone you should not be pursuing romantically.
- *Non-functional compliments*: Functional compliments (such as those that focus on the quality of someone's work) allow you to be warm and pleasant while not communicating more personal interest than you should. By contrast, non-functional compliments communicate a deeper level of personal affirmation and attention. At this stage in your

G4 journey, it is wise to restrict your compliments to functional ones when speaking to people you should not pursue romantically.

- *Touching*: Welcomed, friendly touch reveals a relationship is moving to a more personal level. It expresses that the relationship is closer, more secure, and creates the opportunity for touching to be more than friendly.

- *Prolonged eye contact*: Extended eye contact communicates a deeper level of interest and respect. Eye contact builds a bond. Even in the absence of words, eye contact communicates that you find the person worthy of your full attention. There is no reason to shamefully avoid eye contact, but be cognizant of times when you hold a gaze with someone you should not romantically pursue.

- *Closeness*: Going out of your way to be near another person is a way of expressing affection. Standing closer than is culturally appropriate in conversation communicates a closer-than-casual bond exists in that relationship.

  ► **Reflection:** Has flirting contributed to your sexual sin? If a lack of social interaction or social timidity have fueled your struggle with lust, do not become preoccupied with these points. However, if being flirtatious has contributed to your temptation, be mindful about avoiding these behaviors.

6. **Avoid consuming alcohol or drugs.** This point is about sexual integrity, not sobriety. Avoiding sexual sin requires self-control. Alcohol or other drugs impair self-control. For this reason, it is unwise to partake of drugs and alcohol while you are striving to grow in self-control.

   ► **Reflection:** Has the use of alcohol or drugs contributed to your struggle with sexual integrity? If so, when and how?

7. **Limit interaction with people who exhibit these patterns.** If you have friends who regularly engage in the things we recommend you avoid, it would be wise for you to limit your interaction with them. Overcoming sexual sin requires more than breaking a habit;

it requires changing a lifestyle. This will likely result in changes to
your sphere of friends.

> ▶ **Reflection:** Based on this point, who do you need to limit
> your interaction with? Who tempts you by their example to
> do the things mentioned above?

> ▶ **Read 1 Corinthians 15:33–34.** These are strong words that
> have direct implications for how much you interact with the
> people you listed. Many would object, "But wouldn't God
> want me to be a part of reaching these indi-
> viduals? Isn't that the loving thing to do?"
> The loving thing to do is to be an example of
> the freedom that Christ can provide and the
> choices necessary to pursue that freedom. You
> don't love them well by making their life seem
> okay or sabotaging your own growth toward
> sexual integrity. You love them by being a light
> on a hill (Matthew 5:14–16). If they want to
> take the same journey, invite them to be a part
> of your G4 group.

Overcoming
sexual sin
requires more
than breaking a
habit; it requires
changing a
lifestyle.

FOUR WAYS TO CULTIVATE RELATIONAL PATTERNS OF HONOR

The previous section was about eliminating dishonor. This one is about
cultivating honor in your relationships. If we're not careful, we can
confuse isolation—removing opportunities for lust—with pursuing
honor in relationships. Becoming a hermit who has no impact on the
world may displease God as much as sexual sin.

> ▶ **Read Matthew 22:37–40.** Notice that Jesus says the entire Bible
> depends upon these two positive commands (v. 40). The Bible is
> not primarily built on negative commands (i.e., what we should
> avoid). As you begin to restructure your life, this will be import-
> ant for you to remember. You are not emptying your life—that
> is, you're not primarily focused on stopping certain behaviors.
> Instead, as you will see more and more in the remainder of your
> G4 journey, you are allowing God to restore the holes sin created
> and give you a full life (John 10:10).

In this section we will look at patterns of honor that apply to every relationship. In the next section, we will look at patterns of honor in marriage.

1. **See people as real people.** View members of the other gender as people rather than objects of pleasure. When we lust, we view people as created for our pleasure rather than God's glory. When you are tempted to lust, remind yourself of the roles and relationships in the other person's life.

    > When you are at the mall and notice an attractive woman, look at her face and notice if she is tired. Observe the packages she is carrying and think, "I bet she's a great mom." Make the woman a person and give her a life. . . . One of my clients, after seeing a great body and struggling with lust, asks himself, "I wonder if she knows Jesus?" Giving her a spirit and praying for her gets him back on track. —Doug Rosenau[3]

    > ▶ **Reflection:** What would be the most natural ways for you to humanize the people you are prone to lust after?

2. **Envision love in a real-life story.** As we stated in Step 3, sometimes the story of lust is as tempting as the person we lust after. This is especially true if your motive for lust is to escape. Romance-focused media, even with nonerotic storylines, is fantasy and separate from real life with real struggles. Therefore, it can exacerbate lust. Lust is love minus life. That is why lust is never satisfying for long—it has no substance. If you find this kind of entertainment erodes your ability to be content in real relationships, consider reducing how much of this media you consume. Instead, envision love as part of real life.

    > Our view of sex becomes detached from relationship and intimacy. Sex in porn is just a physical activity, nothing more. But real sex, sex as God intended, is the celebration and climax—quite literally—of a relationship. Godly sex is part of a package that includes talking together, sharing together, deciding together, crying

together, working together, laughing together and forgiving each other. Orgasm comes at the end of a process
that began with offering a compliment, doing the chores,
recalling your day, unburdening your heart, tidying the
house. . . . If you have sex while disregarding intimacy
or unresolved conflict, then that sex will be bad in both
senses of the word: poor quality and ungodly. —Tim
Chester[4]

▶ **Reflection:** Look at the list of actions in Tim Chester's quote.
How can you begin to incorporate these themes and expectations into the way you envision love and romance?

3. **Learn real friendship.** Friendship is more than personal entertainment in the company of others. Real friendship is a give-and-
take, serve-and-be-served relationship. Sometimes friendship is
incredibly fun. Other times friendship is sacrificial or mundane.
If we avoid this reality in our friendships, we will certainly dismiss
it in romantic relationships. Every friendship is an opportunity to
purify our understanding of meaningful relationships.

▶ **Read these one-another passages:** Romans 12:10, 16; 14:13;
15:7, 14; 1 Corinthians 12:25; 2 Corinthians 10:12, 13:11;
Galatians 5:13–15; Colossians 3:9, 13, 16; 1 Thessalonians
4:18; 5:11–15; Hebrews 3:12–14; 10:24–25; James 5:9, 16;
1 Peter 1:22; 4:8–10; 5:5; 1 John 1:7; 4:7. Make a list of the
verbs that come before the phrase "one another." Passages
like this are a collage of what God intends Christian friendships to be like.

▶ **Exercise:** Take your list from the passages above and make it
a scavenger hunt. Be mindful when you have opportunities
to fulfill one of these commands. As you do, pay attention
to the type of satisfaction you feel. Note how it is different
from the experience of lust. By doing so, create an appetite
for wholesome satisfaction in real friendships.

4. **Cultivate same-gendered friendships.** As you cultivate an appetite for real friendships, begin with friendships without romantic

draw. In your initial foray into these more meaningful friendships, it is wise to remove the confounding variable of romantic interest. It will be easier to learn wholesome satisfaction if you don't immediately mix them with a sense of romantic attraction.

Between now and Step 8, cultivating these types of friendships will become a growing point of emphasis. We want to replace hollow, self-indulgent relationships with solid, wholesome friendships. You will learn how to engage your friends more meaningfully as we proceed. For now, begin identifying who these people are.

> View members of the other gender as people rather than objects of pleasure.

▶ **Reflection:** Which same-gendered people in your life would make good friends?

RESTORING HONOR IN MARRIAGE

Sex was made for marriage; marriage was not made for sex. It is similar to saying garages were made for cars, but cars were not made for garages. Lust makes all of life about sex. Often, after a prolonged struggle with sexual sin, the hardest place for sex to take its appropriate size and priority is in marriage. But unless this change occurs, we impose oversized expectations for sex and romance on marriage. Doing so damages a marriage, even though marriage is the appropriate place for sex.

In this section, we will cover three points that are important to marital restoration or the proper anticipation of marriage after a struggle with sexual sin. These points are (1) marital restoration is not marital enrichment; (2) marital sex is not a lust replacement; and (3) you need to keep your spouse informed.

Marital Restoration Is Not Marital Enrichment

It is important for you and your spouse to differentiate marital restoration and marital enrichment. If we conflate restoration and enrichment, we assume that when we stop sinning, our spouse should be fine. That is the equivalent of saying that once the vehicle comes to a complete stop after a car wreck, it should be fully operational and ready for the next road trip, or that the wounds of all passengers should be healed. By contrast, marriage restoration involves doing hard but necessary things to fix a marriage that is broken. Marriage enrichment involves doing nice, romantic things to refine a marriage that is in working order. *False Love* and *True Betrayal* (the complement to this study for your spouse) are marriage restoration resources. You have been working toward fixing things that your sin broke.

As you complete these restoration materials, you should approach your spouse and express your desire to begin marital enrichment—that is, working on the areas of marital weakness you discovered during this study. Honor your spouse by going at their pace. If your spouse says, "I'm not ready for that yet," thank them for their honesty and be patient.

> ▶ **Reflection:** Have you inadvertently conflated marital restoration and marital enrichment? If so, what type of marriage enrichment behaviors did you try to engage in before your spouse was ready? What impact did this have on your spouse?

Marital Sex Is Not a Lust Replacement

Marriage was not intended to satiate lust. That mindset would dishonor your spouse and God's design for marriage. You want to view sex as a celebration of a relationship marked by honor, instead of an appetite that focuses on your personal fulfillment. Sex is an activity meant to strengthen a marriage, not a demand that erodes trust via selfishness.

> Consider the example of the sex addict who never engages in sexual activity with anyone except his wife yet uses sex with his spouse as an escape from intimacy, not as an expression of it. In this case, the sex addict treats his spouse simply as a body and not as a spirit. Here, sex, although it is with a spouse, is really not different than masturbating. . . . The question is whether or not sex is an expression of intimacy or an escape from it. —Mark Laaser[5]

> ▶ **Reflection:** How are you still prone to treat sex as an appetite rather than an expression of love? How can you become more servant-minded in the way you think about romance and sex?

Hint: This has more to do with how you serve and honor your spouse outside the bedroom.

You Need to Keep Your Spouse Informed

We have already said that your spouse should not be your primary accountability partner. While this is still true, we also said your spouse should not be kept in the dark. You do not have to ask whether your spouse is wondering about your integrity or fidelity. They are. Honor this concern by giving your spouse regular updates on your progress. This is an act of love as you put their peace of mind ahead of your personal comfort.

That raises the question, How long should I provide my spouse with updates on how I'm doing? Answer: Do this until they say, "I trust you. There is no need to update me again unless you are facing temptation or have fallen. If I have concerns or fears, I will ask." This is a sign that your investment in the *False Love* study has demonstrated enough consistency and integrity to give your spouse peace of mind. Pray for that time to come, but wait for it patiently.

CLOSING THOUGHTS ON HONOR

This part of Step 6 has been about restoring honor in your relationships. By way of metaphor, *honor* is a broad term that encompasses sexual integrity in the same way that *healthiness* is a broad term that encompasses dieting if we're overweight. At this point in your journey, you best preserve sexual integrity by aiming for the broader goal of seeking honor in all your relationships. This helps you desexualize the work you're doing, which is important when you're battling lust.

Be encouraged that you've reached this point in your journey. It is an important and significant marker. As with any marker on a journey like this, your ability to be encouraged without letting your guard down is pivotal. Many of us know what it's like to pass a midterm and think that means we can neglect studying for the final. That's foolish. But passing the midterm should give us confidence that if we continue to prepare like we have to this point, we will do well. That is the kind of encouragement you should take from this marker.

G4 GROUP DISCUSSION: STEP 6, PART THREE

As you discuss this material in G4 group, these questions are meant to facilitate a more honest and beneficial dialogue about this material. Anyone is free to respond to whichever questions they choose.

Experienced Members

- What secondary emotion was most difficult for you to express as a primary emotion? How did learning to be honest about your primary emotions help you battle lust?
- If you are married, which of the final points on honor in marriage made the biggest impact on your marriage?

New Members

- Do you have relationships that pull you down and you need to create more distance from?
- How did Tim Chester's quote challenge the way you think about sex and intimacy?
- How can we pray for you?

Everyone

- Which of the seven ways to remove relational dishonor is most important for you to implement?
- What are ways you've learned to see people as real people?
- Have you experienced a significant setback or victory since last meeting that you should tell the group?

STEP 6
PART FOUR

STRENGTHENING YOUR SOUL

The video for this part of Step 6 can be found at: bradhambrick.com/falselove6p4.

In this part of Step 6, we are going to examine spiritual disciplines that can strengthen our pursuit of integrity. You will find that as you've gone through this study, you have already been incorporating most of them. However, at this stage in your journey, you want to make sure these are part of your life rhythms and not merely a side product of studying through *False Love*.

Also, we want to acknowledge we do not engage spiritual disciplines primarily for therapeutic reasons; we engage them to know and enjoy God. However, when engaged well, these disciplines have significant therapeutic benefits. That is the equivalent of saying, if you're married, you don't date your spouse to save money on counseling. But if you invest time and energy into your marriage, it does save time and money lost to unnecessary relational strain.

SPIRITUAL DISCIPLINES TO EMBRACE

Some benefits can be generally ascribed to particular disciplines. That is what we want to explore in this part of Step 6. We want to answer the question, "What unique benefits does each spiritual discipline bring to our G4 journey and life after G4?"

Bible Study

Sexual sin embeds itself in the rhythms of our life. Our routines become highly disciplined and sacrificial in the pursuit of our vice. Integrity requires a comparable level of being embedded in the rhythms of our life. Your sexual sin grew stronger as you fed it daily with time, attention, and practice. Your spiritual life will grow the same way as you infuse it with consistent and intentional Bible study.

How much of the struggle with sexual sin is the bad content in our thinking (commonly referred to in recovery circles as "stinkin' thinkin'")? This folksy adage reveals the importance of the content and tone of our thinking. Christians have long emphasized the importance of perpetually renewing our mind (Romans 12:2).

> We do not engage spiritual disciplines primarily for therapeutic reasons. However, when engaged well, these disciplines have significant therapeutic benefits.

What is your pattern of daily Bible intake? This *False Love* study is filled with devotional Bible studies. The purpose of these Bible studies is twofold: (a) to demonstrate the theological foundation for this material, and (b) to get you in the habit of reading the Bible devotionally. If you have been skimming these, begin to engage them more seriously. Use them to learn to study the Bible for personal growth. Also begin to have a time of daily Bible reading that is separate from your G4 study.

- Consider reading one chapter from the book of Proverbs per day.
- Consider reading through the four Gospels—Matthew, Mark, Luke, and John—one chapter per day.

Make a plan. Keep it simple. Become consistent. Allow it to grow over time.

For more guidance on this spiritual discipline, consider the following chapters from these resources on cultivating spiritual disciplines in your life:

- Richard Foster, *Celebration of Discipline: The Path to Spiritual Growth*, chapter 5
- Brad Hambrick, "Four Ways to Read the Bible" (blog available at bradhambrick.com/BibleReading)
- John Ortberg, *The Life You've Always Wanted: Spiritual Disciplines for Ordinary People*, chapter 10
- Donald Whitney, *Spiritual Disciplines for the Christian Life*, chapters 2 and 3.

Prayer and Worship

How much of the struggle with sexual sin results from our thoughts mindlessly wandering toward lust? Our thinking needs a direction to be healthy. Prayer and worship provide direction for our thoughts. Prayer allows our inward thoughts to connect with someone who cares and understands. Worship provides a focal point for our thoughts (God) that is grander than our situation is bad (lust and its consequences). Prayer and worship are ways we can be positively awed by God's goodness and grace, rather than negatively awed by the impact of our sin.

> Christian worship graciously displaces us from being the center of our story and instead incorporates us into the story of God. —Kent Dunnington[1]

What is your daily habit of prayer? Chances are fantasy has replaced prayer. When stress arises, you turn to the romantic or erotic instead of God. Prayer can be a powerful means of change for these mental reflexes. Initially, start with simple, brief, conversational prayers that emerge from the events around you. The following are some examples:

- Has your day stalled? Begin a prayer with, "I'm bored," and talk with God like a friend.
- Are you frustrated? Begin a prayer with, "This is hard," and talk with God like someone who wants help.
- Are you tempted? Begin a prayer with, "Thank you for being with me," and talk to God like he's present.
- Whatever you're feeling, turn it into a prayer prompt. Focus especially on those emotions most closely associated with the motives you identified in Step 3.

Often Christians get caught up in how long they pray. They feel defeated and say, "I couldn't even pray for five minutes without my thoughts drifting to someone else." For now, focus on how many micro-prayers you can infuse into your day. If you bring seventeen hard moments to God in a day, don't worry about the cumulative duration. Get in the habit of bringing the meaningful parts of your life to God in prayer and the duration will take care of itself.

▶ **Action Step:** Begin to have regular, down-to-earth conversations with God. Don't get caught up in fancy words, just talk with God about your day as you live it.

For guidance on this spiritual discipline, consider the following chapters from these classic books:

> Chances are that fantasy has become the replacement for prayer. When stress arises, turn to God.

- Richard Foster, *Celebration of Discipline: The Path to Spiritual Growth*, chapters 3 and 11
- Paul Miller, *A Praying Life: Connecting with God in a Distracting World*
- John Ortberg, *The Life You've Always Wanted: Spiritual Disciplines for Ordinary People*, chapter 4
- Donald Whitney, *Spiritual Disciplines for the Christian Life*, chapters 4 and 5

Silence, Stillness, and Meditation

How much of our struggle with lust is our inability to rein in our thoughts or tolerate the discomfort of being alone or stressed? Silence, stillness, and meditation are disciplines that tame the wild horse of our thoughts and emotions. They are practices advocated by Christians for centuries because of the benefits for the life and character of believers.

▶ **Action Step:** When you feel disrupted, pause. Take a deep breath. Be still and quiet your mind for thirty seconds. Allow this to be an act of faith that shows your trust that God cares about you and is at work in whatever is bothering you. Reengage whatever needs to be done next with the benefits of this stillness.

For guidance on this spiritual discipline, consider the following chapters from these books:

- Richard Foster, *Celebration of Discipline: The Path to Spiritual Growth*, chapters 2 and 7
- John Ortberg, *The Life You've Always Wanted: Spiritual Disciplines for Ordinary People*, chapter 5
- Esther Smith, *A Still and Quiet Mind: Twelve Strategies for Changing Unwanted Thoughts*
- Donald Whitney, *Spiritual Disciplines for the Christian Life*, chapter 10

Journaling

How much of the struggle with sexual sin is the seemingly pointless disconnectedness of day-to-day life? Life can easily begin to feel like a bad novel where one page has little to do with the page before it and the story is going nowhere. Events keep happening, but they don't seem to contribute anything. This is what led Socrates to say, "The unexamined life is not worth living." Journaling is a common way to consistently step back and gain a more holistic perspective on life.

> ▶ **Reflection:** How have your written responses to the prompts in this G4 study aided your growth, been healthy for your emotions, and cultivated a greater sense of purpose in your life? If this facet of G4 has blessed you, be intentional about continuing it after you graduate.

For guidance on this spiritual discipline, consider the following resources:

- Brad Hambrick, "Using a Personal Journal for Spiritual Growth" (resource available at www.bradhambrick.com/journal)
- Donald Whitney, *Spiritual Disciplines for the Christian Life*, chapter 11

CONCLUSION

Remember Step 6 is a buffet. The four parts of Step 6 have offered you a multitude of potential strategies to implement. No one could implement them all and maintain a healthy life. The intent is for you to select the strategies that best fit your life now and to have an arsenal of strategies to select from as your life changes.

For this step to be effective, you need to answer the following three questions:

> ▶ **Which strategies** are more strategic for my continued progress? (Pick three)
> ▶ **Why** is each strategy I selected important for my progress?
> ▶ **What are the indicators** that this strategy is having its intended impact on my life?

If you have trouble identifying what you want to begin with, ask your fellow G4 members who are going through this study with you what seems like the best fit. This is a low-pressure choice. You can't really go wrong. Pick three. Implement them consistently for a couple of months. Then you can evaluate them. The practice of being consistent and working toward a goal will be valuable, even if you decide later that a different strategy would be more advantageous.

G4 GROUP DISCUSSION: STEP 6, PART FOUR

As you discuss this material in G4 group, these questions are meant to facilitate a more honest and beneficial dialogue about this material. Anyone is free to respond to whichever questions they choose.

Experienced Members

- Which spiritual discipline has been most beneficial for your progress?
- How do you help prevent your spiritual disciplines from becoming lifeless and performed out of duty?

New Members

- Did anything about this part of Step 6 come across as "just read your Bible and everything will be okay"?
- Which of the benefits described for each spiritual discipline counters the factors that contribute significantly to your struggle with lust?
- How can we pray for you?

Everyone

- How does the metaphor of dates and marriage counseling help you understand the importance of focusing your spiritual disciplines on cultivating a relationship with God more than focusing on the therapeutic benefits of that relationship?
- Of all the strategies provided in Step 6, what are your current top three and why have you chosen them?
- Have you experienced a significant setback or victory since last meeting that you should tell the group?

STEP 7
IMPLEMENT
the new structure pervasively
with humility and flexibility.

At the end of this step, I want to be able to say . . .

"Implementing a plan is harder than creating a plan.
Trying to live out my plan has taught me
more about myself, my sin, and my Savior. As I
have had victory, the old expressions of sexual sin
have taken new forms [describe]. Here are
the unexpected challenges I faced [list], how I failed
[list], where I succeeded [list], what I learned [list],
and how God was faithful [list]."

STEP 7
PART ONE

RESPONDING TO RELAPSE

The video for this part of Step 7 can be found at: bradhambrick.com/falselove7p1.

A s you arrive at Step 7, the momentum of change has probably already fluctuated several times. Getting started was hard. It felt like an uphill battle. Old patterns of life didn't want to let go of you, and you didn't want to admit they had a hold on you. Forsaking sexual sin can feel like betraying a friend; breakups are never easy even when they're good and needed.

But honesty with self, others, and God has a great way of building momentum. You began to let go of the weights of sin that clung to you so you could run free (Hebrews 12:1). This second phase is almost always exciting. When there are so many ways that your life can be healthier, it can bring a great sense of hope and progress.

In the third phase, the one we're starting now, life restructuring may begin to feel more like work again. *Implementation* is not an exciting word or process. Lasting change happens in incremental units and mundane moments. Change begins to impact moments that feel less relevant to your battle for sexual integrity. The freedom you've gained tempts you to think you can risk a few of your previous bad habits.

In Step 7, we will focus on these three things:

1. Learning how to respond to relapse
2. Identifying markers of progress
3. Assessing life holistically to identify remaining areas of needed change

Note: It is recommended that you give at least two months to this step. You will need to see how your plan responds to the changes of settings, relationships, and emotions that happen over months, rather than days or a couple of weeks. It is easy to move through Step 7 too quickly and not give it the attention it requires.

DISCUSSING RELAPSE

The word *relapse* may bring many thoughts: *Is every slip a relapse? Does every bad choice mean I'm starting over? How can I not expect perfection for the rest of my life without making excuses that make it easier to slip back into destructive behaviors?* You can see why relapse is such a difficult subject.

> Forsaking sexual sin can feel like betraying a friend; breakups are never easy even when they're good and needed.

On one hand, you can expect to relapse many times in the journey. Learning from failure is part of the process. On the other hand, we don't want to expect to fail. We want to face every temptation with the expectation that we'll rely on God to make healthy, God-honoring choices. We want to learn to live wisely in this tension rather than picking sides of the argument. With that said, here are seven expectations from G4 regarding relapse:

1. We will face relapse.
2. Relapse is the recurrence of any self-destructive behavior related to our desired change.
3. Dishonesty and hiding are more dangerous than relapse.
4. Dishonesty and hiding are the difference between a relapse slip (short-term) and relapse slide (long-term).
5. Relapse begins to end when honesty begins.
6. We are more likely to be honest about something we've openly discussed.
7. We discuss relapse not to excuse or predict it, but to place ourselves in a position for a healthy response.

To help prevent the first two expectations—facing relapse and recurring destructive behaviors—from derailing our progress, we will use a four-phase model for understanding relapse.[1] It is important to keep in mind that experiencing an early phase in the cycle does not make the latter phases inevitable. For this reason, we will look at each phase separately and ask two questions: (a) How do I realize I'm in this phase? and (b) What should I do at this phase to exit the relapse cycle?

Phase One: Change Fatigue

"I just want a break from working these steps . . . having accountability . . . thinking about temptation . . . etc." This is the mild, passive-aggressive defiance of fatigue. It may mean that due our present progress, we are downplaying how severe our struggle with sexual sin was in the past. Minimizing sets us up to make unwise, risky choices and resent those who caution us against those choices. Or it may mean that we're trying to do too much—that we've added too much to our schedule too fast. This makes us feel like the people who caution us just aren't being practical.

With this in mind, learn to pay attention to your unpleasant emotions: irritation, fatigue, stress, insecurity, loneliness, defensiveness, etc. These dispositions are often gateways to complacency. When you experience these dispositions, reach out to a member of your support network. Being alone with these emotions can be as dangerous as being alone with your computer or adultery partner.

Honesty and listening are the two best responses to the complacency phase. We need to be humbly honest about the internal resistance we feel. Don't give fake, nice answers to get people off your back. We need to listen to the concerns brought to us. It is likely that others will see the yellow flags we want to ignore.

Phase Two: Convenient Confusion

Some people say, "Worldliness is what makes sin look normal and righteousness look strange." The further we get into temptation, the more this dynamic affects our thinking and the more we become confused or resistant to God-honoring choices. You begin to view healthy choices as an unnecessary burden. You begin to view unhealthy choices as moments of freedom. You begin to view supportive friends as people who don't understand and expect too much.

In the confusion phase, we are usually still committed enough to integrity to say things like, "I know I should think/feel this, but . . ." The experience of confusion should make us humble, not confident; it should prompt us to move toward trusted people, not pull away from them. If your instincts are the opposite of this, consider it a major red flag.

Honesty and increasing accountability to stay away from compromising situations are the best responses to confusion. If you were dizzy, you wouldn't walk near a cliff. The same principle applies here. Call your G4 group leader, pastor, or a trusted friend and say something like, "I can tell my thinking is off. I may not want to hear what you have to say, but we need to talk."

> The experience of confusion should make us humble, not confident; it should prompt us to move toward trusted people, not pull away from them.

Phase Three: "Acceptable" Hedging

We begin to fall back into viewing sexual sin as a form of relief and think, *I deserve my [self-destructive behavior].* The longer it has been since we acted out—the longer it's been since we've felt the consequences of our choices—the easier it can be to believe this thought pattern. Frequent warning signs of hedging are the following:

- You fantasize about "the good old days" when you engaged in sexual sin.
- You believe that you can act out again but control it this time (overconfidence).
- Your emotions become moody, and your attitude becomes selfish.
- You begin to pull away from or neglect friends who have been part of pursuing sexual integrity.
- You are defensive when someone brings up changes in your mood, attitude, or actions.
- You begin to neglect your outlets for healthy fun or enjoy them less.
- You begin to engage healthy interests in excessive ways (i.e., excessive exercise, compulsive cleaning, etc.).

Honesty and transparency are the best responses to compromise. At this point, you are hiding things again. That should scare you. Hiding never ends well. When we hide our choices, it transforms how we think. The people we hide our choices from are seen as being against us. But these are the people who love us most and want the best for us. That is why the courage to be honest by being transparent is essential to prevent compromise from becoming a catastrophe.

Phase Four: Inevitable Demise

Destructive choices destroy. There is no way around that. When we fail to acknowledge how we start hedging (phase three), some life crisis will eventually get our attention. Don't allow shame or pride to prevent you from being honest about your choices.

While our goal has been to interrupt the relapse cycle before it reaches the phase of life-altering consequences, the earlier in the declining process that we acknowledge what is happening, the better it will be. Until we are honest, things really can get worse. Don't believe the lie that they can't.

Honesty that is willing to accept consequences is the best response to a catastrophe. We often fail to be honest about this final phase because we are trying to manage or mitigate the consequences of our choices. That is as futile as trying to put out a grease fire with water. It spreads the problem. What puts out the fire of a catastrophe is honesty. It removes the oxygen of deceit.

▶ **Read 1 Corinthians 10:13.** "God will not let you be tempted beyond your ability" doesn't just mean the type or intensity of temptation, but also means at any point in the temptation cycle. Too often we conceptualize a fictional point of no return in the buildup of lust. If a point of no return exists, it is the point at which we decide not to be honest with God, ourselves, and others. The grace of God means there is always hope in honesty. When God promises to provide a "way of escape," it refers not to the removal of all consequences, but the opportunity for redemption and restoration to begin. Restoration requires acknowledging the brokenness. That is as true for every relapse as it was at the beginning of your G4 journey.

G4 GROUP DISCUSSION: STEP 7, PART ONE

As you discuss this material in G4 group, these questions are meant to facilitate a more honest and beneficial dialogue about this material. Anyone is free to respond to whichever questions they choose.

Experienced Members

- What are some of your most frustrating experiences with relapse, and what did you learn from them?
- What indicators of relapse in your life are most important for you to take seriously?

New Members

- How many times have you tried to stop your sexual sin? Has that discouraged you from trying again?
- How has your experience proven the saying, "Worldliness is what makes sin look normal and righteousness look strange"?
- How can we pray for you?

Everyone

- What aspects of confusion (phase two) are you experiencing that we should talk about?
- How did thinking about 1 Corinthians 10:13 in light of each phase of the relapse cycle change the way you applied this verse to your life?
- Have you experienced a significant setback or victory since last meeting that you should tell the group?

STEP 7
PART TWO

MEASURING MULTIDIMENSIONAL PROGRESS

The video for this part of Step 7 can be found at: bradhambrick.com/falselove7p2.

Measuring progress is tricky for many reasons. Imagine it like trying to measure the ocean tide. Do you measure at the furthest point the water reaches? Do you measure the midpoint of each wave? Do you measure it by the point in the sand that is always underwater? Does the measure change if the tide is going out versus when it is coming in? Change with a life-dominating struggle with sexual sin requires considering the dynamic (i.e., ever-moving) aspects of the change process.

Measuring progress with a major lifestyle is an attempt to measure something fluid and dynamic. You can monitor behavior; did you look at pornography? You can measure temptation; did you consider texting your adultery partner? You can focus on supplemental behaviors; have you been honest and transparent? Is refraining from sexual sin with a defensive attitude toward supportive friends a good or bad thing? These questions help us see that we need a multidimensional approach to how we think about progress.

Measuring progress tends to measure performance over dependence. This tendency can easily begin to undermine the God-reliance stressed throughout this G4 curriculum, as if we are going to master sexual integrity. Thinking we've arrived or that we've done so well that we don't need other people is a significant yellow flag (if not red flag). Healthy growth involves joyful dependence on God and healthy interdependence with other people.

Measuring progress can foster shame when there is some type of regression. How we handle regression is pivotal to establishing lasting change, hence the previous section on relapse. We need a view of progress that gives credit for our response to failures. Without this, our definition of progress fosters a mindset of hiding and disingenuousness.

PROGRESS INDICATORS

David Powlison gives seven indicators of that good progress.[1] Allow these measures to give you a more robust understanding of progress than merely counting the number of days since you gave into sexual sin. As you read these, consider how each point helps you see and maintain progress even when you are tempted. The following bold points are from Powlison, and the G4 application follows each point.

1. **Decrease in the frequency of sin.** Progress means we sin less. As you have worked through this G4 curriculum, there should be noticeable and quantifiable decreases in the frequency of your sin. Whatever dimensions we add to our definition of progress, we are not detracting from or minimizing this one.

2. **Repenting more quickly.** Progress means we respond to temptation and relapse differently. Prompt repentance is the key to stopping a relapse. No longer will you give into the mindset, "If I've already been bad, I might as well enjoy it." We should now be convinced, "The quicker I am honest, the freer I will be."

3. **Change in the battleground.** Progress means you see an advance in your battle against sin from behaviors and belief to its core fortress—your heart commitments. These changes should excite you. This realization is what allowed Paul to say he was the "chief" of sinners without shame (1 Timothy 1:15 KJV). He was excited to take his battle with sin to its core. While each new battleground may require different strategies and time durations to win, there should be joy as you see God's kingdom penetrating new territory in your soul.

4. **Having a greater sense of need for Christ.** Progress without persistently attributing it to reliance upon Christ degenerates into pride. Pride is the gateway to a multitude of temptations. The point

is not trying to predict what form every new temptation will take, but remaining humble and joyfully aware of your need for Christ in order to live a satisfying life.

5. **Increased accountability and honesty.** Progress means that you do not need a reason to be honest and things do not have to be "that bad" for you to have accountability. In many ways, this variable is one of the primary, practical expressions of humility. Humble people refuse to fight sin alone and refuse to trust their own hearts apart from the community of caring Christian friends (Hebrews 3:12–14).

6. **Not responding to difficulty by seeking sexual sin.** Difficulty is the time when progress is most clear. When we forget this, we become discouraged by difficulty and this discouragement adds to our temptation. Recognize that when difficulty comes (i.e., conflict, stress, setbacks, illness, etc.), it will be a time when your progress will be most evident. Realizing this should help you maintain the will to persevere during these challenges.

7. **Learning to love and consider the interest of real people.** This is the epitome of progress because it is the fulfillment of the whole law of God (Galatians 6:2). The opposite of sexual sin is not merely integrity. The opposite of sexual sin is the ability to care for real people and a willingness to be known by others in the ups and downs of real life. We no longer lust after or feel inferior to other people; we seek to love them. We don't force them into our romantic narrative and stereotypes; we seek to get to know them for who they really are.

    ▶ **Reflection:** Think of specific examples of when and how each of these indicators of change has been present in your life during the last three months. Give thanks for God's grace in each example. Also, see in each example the fulfillment of God's promise to be faithful and never abandon you in hard times (Deuteronomy 31:6; John 14:18).

These seven markers focus primarily on progress during the moment of temptation. They treat each temptation as an independent event. This is a helpful perspective. It allows us to look at a moment of struggle and ask, "How did I do?" It is also helpful to look at larger units of time and ask, "How am I doing?" That is the focus of the sound wave image we will consider next.

CHANGE COMPARED TO A SOUND WAVE

A sound wave can be measured based on three dimensions: intensity, duration, and frequency. How loud was the sound? How long did the sound last? How often did the sound occur? To help you visualize this point, consider the illustration below:

> Difficulty is the time when progress is most clear.

- Intensity (height: A to B)
- Duration (width: Y to Z)
- Frequency (peak to peak: 1 to 2)

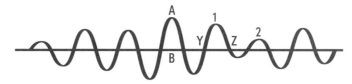

Figure 5. Change and Sound Wave Comparison

Temptation can be measured in comparable categories. This gives you three more ways that you can begin to gauge your progress. Is your temptation *less intense*? Does your temptation last for *briefer periods of time*? Are your temptations *less frequent*? Your Step 3 journals should provide an objective basis for this assessment.

To provide some encouragement, consider the following "Life Disruption Score" (LDS). LDS is an arbitrary statistic, but it highlights a valid point. Let's assume that the intensity, duration, and frequency of your temptations were maxed out on a 1 to 10 scale. That would create a maximum LDS score of 1,000.

10 (intensity) x 10 (duration) x 10 (frequency) = 1,000

Now let's assume that you decrease the impact of each variable by only two increments. How much do you think that would improve your LDS score?

8 (intensity) x 8 (duration) x 8 (frequency) = _____ (yes, do the math)

Are you surprised at what a small amount of progress in each area can do? This isn't just a math trick. We tend to think about change by considering a terrible event and thinking, *If only I had done* everything *differently!* That equates progress with perfection. All-or-nothing thinking is defeatist thinking. We don't want to think that way anymore. The sound wave metaphor allows us to see progress as temptation shrinks (as opposed to it vanishing).

Consider your last episode of succumbing to temptation, lying, hiding, and the subsequent fallout. What choices could you have made to move from level 10 to level 8 in that situation? At how many points did your conscience temporarily prompt you to change, but you thought, *What's the point now?* How would those events have transpired differently if you saw the value of making a level 10 to level 8 change? If we see the value in making these changes, we are more likely to make them.

Your goal in this part of Step 7 is to see more dimensions of what progress is. The value in seeing multiple dimensions of progress is in increasing your motivation to make healthy, God-honoring choices in moments of temptation or in the early phases of relapse. It is always possible to do the next healthy, God-honoring thing. And it is always worth it.

▶ **Read Mark 8:22–25.** This miracle is unique because it happens in stages. The man starts blind (v. 22). Then his vision was partially restored (v. 24). Finally, his vision was fully restored (v. 25). In Jesus's ministry, miracles were often called signs because they were meant to point us to who God is and how God works. This miracle is a sign (i.e., picture) of how God works in our life. We will miss the point of the miracle if we think, *If God is working in my life, I'd be fully delivered. This step-by-step stuff means he's not working in me.* God often works incrementally in our lives. The work that God began, he promises to finish (Philippians 1:6). He promises to finish this work as we continue to remain invested in his agenda with our life (Philippians 2:12).

G4 GROUP DISCUSSION: STEP 7, PART TWO

As you discuss this material in G4 group, these questions are meant to facilitate a more honest and beneficial dialogue about this material. Anyone is free to respond to whichever questions they choose.

Experienced Members

- Can you remember a time when an all-or-nothing mindset toward progress disrupted your recovery?
- Which of Powlison's seven indicators of progress was most impactful in your recovery?

New Members

- Before coming to G4, how would you have defined progress in recovery?
- What is your response to the statement, "It is always possible to do the next healthy, God-honoring thing. And it is always worth it"?
- How can we pray for you?

> It is always possible to do the next healthy, God-honoring thing. And it is always worth it.

Everyone

- How did the devotion on Mark 8 help you understand the value of this part of Step 7?
- What is your response to the statement: "The opposite of sexual sin is not merely integrity. The opposite of sexual sin is the ability to care for real people and a willingness to be known by others in the ups and downs of real life"?
- Have you experienced a significant setback or victory since last meeting that you should tell the group?

STEP 7
PART THREE

ASSESSING LIFE HOLISTICALLY

The video for this part of Step 7 can be found at: bradhambrick.com/falselove7p3.

Now that we have a more holistic picture of what progress looks like, we want to discern where we should expect to find and cultivate it. During the early steps in this journey, it is apparent what progress is and where to find it. In the later steps, these things can be less obvious, but they are no less important. Incomplete work in the latter steps is like building a beautiful deck on your home and not sealing the wood. There is reason for short-term celebration, but the lasting benefits will be compromised.

Take a moment and visualize a mountain in your mind's eye. What do you see? Chances are that the picture in your mind is a snow-capped peak. This is the part of a mountain that captures our attention. But these peaks don't float. There are massive amounts of rock, dirt, and trees under those peaks. Similarly, when we think of our battle against sexual sin, we think of the worst moments. Our attention is captured by these "peak moments" of pinnacle destructive experiences that emerged from our sinful choices. But these moments don't float. Under those moments are many other unhealthy habits and values, missing skills, points of pride, and insecurity. In this part of Step 7, we want to identify these and root them out.

For this assessment, we will examine the who, when, where, and what of your sin. Our goal is larger than just the absence of sexual sin. We want to begin to make our life as inhospitable for sin as possible by removing patterns of behavior that are not God-honoring or healthy.

INSPECTION AREA ONE: *WHO?*

Spouse

If you are married, the role of your spouse has likely changed several times on your G4 journey. At first, they were the person most hurt by your sin and with whom you were most deceptive. Then, your spouse became the person to whom you wisely deferred choices in your pursuit of integrity. As an act of honor, you chose what provided them with the most security. During this middle phase, your spouse frequently asked questions about your actions as they regained a sense of trust. Now we hope to begin moving toward a "new normal" phase, where your history of sexual sin has an ever-diminishing influence on how the two of you think about your marriage. Before we do that, we will ask again about your honesty.

> ► **Reflection:** Have you been completely honest with your spouse? Are you currently living transparently with your spouse?

Often around Step 7 a couple transitions from marital restoration toward marital enrichment—that is, from fixing a marriage broken by sexual sin to refining a functional marriage that has been honored with integrity. For marital enrichment guidance, you may find *Creating a Gospel-Centered Marriage* enrichment seminars helpful for marital foundations, communication, finances, decision-making, and intimacy (available at bradhambrick.com/gcm).[1]

> ► **Reflection:** If married, what aspects of enrichment warrant attention in your marriage?

At this stage in your G4 journey, marriage enrichment and learning to manage life and conflict better will be an important part of your continued growth.

Individuals

Are there particular people who trigger heightened temptations for you?

> ► **Exercise:** Make a list of people who are a negative influence on your continued progress.

Sometimes we make unwise choices in a relationship because we feel unsafe (e.g., solicited by a superior at work or blackmailed by someone who has compromising pictures of us). In these cases, we succumb to the temptation to try to manage a greater threat. If safety-level concerns prompt your temptation, seek guidance from law enforcement, a supervisor, teacher, or other suitable authority figure over that relationship. If the relationship does not have a suitable over-seer, then seek the guidance of a pastor or counselor. The book *The Emotionally Destructive Relationship* by Leslie Vernick can also be a helpful resource.

Other times, we make unwise choices in relationships because of insecurity. In these cases, we need to learn how to vocalize those concerns, learn social skills to overcome points of insecurity, and work to become less dependent upon the approval of others. The resources below address various aspects of these concerns.

- Brad Hambrick, *Navigating Destructive Relationships* is a resource in the G4 series for responding to relationships marked by abuse or addiction (bradhambrick.com/destructive)
- Ken Sande, *The Peacemaker: A Biblical Guide to Resolving Personal Conflict*
- Ed Welch, *When People Are Big and God Is Small: Overcoming Peer Pressure, Codependency, and the Fear of Man*

Groups of People

If your temptations are attached to groups of people (i.e., those who have more status, better appearance, or some other marker you deem significant, etc.), you need to examine the motivation and history for that reaction.

> ▶ **Exercise:** List the groups of people who are emotionally disruptive for you.

Generally, temptations prompted by a group can be attributed to (a) an idolatrous overvaluing of certain desirable attributes or social roles, (b) aspects of an abusive personal history that changed your instinctual response to those who remind you of your abusive experience, or (c) a prejudicial response toward that group of people.

▶ **Reflection:** What is it about the groups of people that are disruptive for you and account for their emotional influence?

▶ **Read Galatians 3:28–29.** Strong emotional reactions based upon group identification reveal that we are overvaluing something. Our reaction reveals that our preferences have become a strong measuring system. Part of the emotional and relational freedom the gospel provides comes from the realization that we are all equally valued by God and equally in need of salvation. Our false systems of social hierarchy—believing that some people are better than others because of certain qualities we deem desirable—erodes the freedom given with this truth.

Roles

Sometimes our emotional reactions have less to do with a particular person than with the dynamic of the relationship or the responsibilities we bear in a particular position. If a particular role prevents you from experiencing greater freedom, it is important to discern whether it is because of inadequate training or preparation to fulfill that role or the weight or significance that you place upon that role.

▶ **Reflection:** What roles do you fill that create stress that in turn increases temptation (i.e., parent, spouse, employee, supervisor, confidant, etc.)?

If a lack of training or preparation for a particular role creates the angst that prompts temptation, ask yourself the questions, "What training do I need?" and "How could I begin to pursue it?" Much of this study has prompted you to be proactive toward life struggles rather than trying to escape through fleeting pleasures. Continue being proactive by seeking the training you need to be more comfortable in the role generating stress.

If you are overvaluing a particular role, you will have to wrestle with your priorities and values. Imbalanced priorities will crash even the best of systems. This means that regardless of creating an excellent plan for change in Step 6, you will migrate back toward what you previously knew unless your values change. In this scenario, the insights that you gained in Step 3 about motives will be important focal points for your accountability relationships.

INSPECTION AREA TWO: *WHEN?*

Time of Day/Week/Month

Pay attention to whether temptation emerges at predictable times of the day, week, or month.

> ▶ **Reflection:** Is the struggle harder at regular points in your day, week, or month? If so, what type of rhythm best accounts for this—sleep cycle, workload, moments of solitude when your actions can be hidden, social interaction, mealtimes, financial pay cycles, hormonal cycles, etc.?

If your temptation is linked to biological or time-related rhythms, it would be wise to consult with a physician who could help identify how to regulate the bodily functions that account for these changes.

If your temptations are linked to behavioral or social rhythms, you need to examine your life management systems. How well do you manage time and money? How willing are you to say no to overcommitment? If you find your mismanagement is rooted in bad priorities, which is often the case, then repent and commit to change. If the mismanagement is rooted in ignorance, commit to learning more as well as changing.

Seasons

Seasonal or annual rhythms can also be a source of temptation. Different seasons present different challenges. Summer is hot and people wear more revealing clothes. Thanksgiving, Christmas, and New Year's often include celebrations with substances that lower inhibitions, create stress, and break our life rhythms (which have become a source of accountability and protection). Winter months may bring gray skies and indoor weather, leaving you more prone toward depression and tempted to get an emotional boost from sexual sin.

> ▶ **Reflection:** What seasonal or annual factors increase your temptation?

Seasonal temptations are predictable. Talk with people in your support network about plans to face those temptations.

Occasions of Energy Level Fluctuation

Fatigue impacts temptation. When we're tired, our capacity for self-control is diminished. Also, when we are tired, we often think we deserve a break or reward, and, as we said in Step 3, in moments of weakness we define "reward" as sexual sin. Consider the following questions to help you assess whether your lifestyle is setting you up to have a consistent energy level, thereby reducing your level of temptation:

- Are you managing your life so that you have time and the mental freedom to get adequate sleep?
- Are you eating a healthy diet so that your body has what it needs to be nutritionally balanced?
- Are you getting cardiovascular exercise to help your body eliminate the chemical by-products of stress?
- Are you engaging in activities you enjoy so that your desire for a healthy life remains high?
- Are you using caffeine or other stimulants to offset unhealthy sleep habits?
- Can you thrive for the next decade if you live like you have for the last week or month?

Before/After

Learning to manage anticipation, dread, disappointment, and achievement are important parts of maintaining sexual integrity. Otherwise, the before or after of a significant experience can easily become a source of temptation. These times may include events such as work deadlines, visits to family, interactions involving conflict, time with in-laws, etc. The following points help us see who might be more prone to temptation in certain situations:

- Anticipation—those who do not respond well to uncertainty
- Dread—those who tend to anticipate unpleasant experiences with worry or fear
- Disappointment—those with a perfectionistic bent

- Achievement—those who believe the reward should be self-gratification

> ▶ **Reflection:** Look back over your recent temptation journals. Do any significant before-or-after events contribute to these temptations?

Life Transitions

Major life transitions can also be times of emotional disorientation and times of temptation. Some of these transitions include leaving for college, experiencing an empty nest, working a first or new job, becoming a parent or grandparent, undergoing midlife crisis, and retiring. These experiences leave us unsettled and impact us in at least two ways: (1) they cause us to question our identity, and (2) they make it hard for us to know how we should feel or what our routine should look like.

> ▶ **Reflection:** What upcoming significant life transitions do you need to prepare for?

> ▶ **Read Ecclesiastes 3:1–8.** "For everything there is a season, and a time for every matter under heaven" (v. 1). God is not annoyed that we need to consider how these time factors impact our temptation. He knows we must pay attention to these factors. God invites—even commands—us to make these kinds of assessments (Ephesians 5:16). These evaluations are like a coach thinking through the strategy needed in each quarter or situation of a game, or a chef thinking about the food prep that needs to be done at each stage of the cooking process. It is naive and disruptive to avoid this kind of evaluation.

INSPECTION AREA THREE: *WHERE?*

Home

There are dynamics to homelife that are distinct from other locations. Home is where we get to relax and not be "on" anymore. Home is a place where we keep our stuff and have the most privacy (meaning it is easier to hide things there). Home is often a place where we engage more comfort-seeking behaviors. You can quickly begin to see how home will either be a great protector or contributor to our patterns of sexual sin and why that location is usually not a neutral influence on us.

If your homelife has a significant influence on your sexual sin, ask a friend or a counselor to review your answers to the questions below. Be sure that you are assessing what changes are possible and how to best accomplish them well. If sexual sin has been your normal experience, it is likely that you may overestimate or underestimate the impact of potential changes.

> Home will either be a great protector or contributor to our patterns of sexual sin.

- What aspects of your homelife (routine and physical layout) contribute to your temptation?
- What aspects of your homelife (routine and physical layout) help alleviate your temptation?
- How or when can you refine or alter those aspects that contribute to your temptation?

Work or School

If we are only thinking about areas of direct sexual temptation, we may miss what happens at work and school. At these locations there are subtler influences on our temptation toward sexual sin. Putting too much weight on our success or failure at work or school can have a profound influence on our motivation to pursue sexual integrity. But these indirect influences may include factors that make us more or less motivated to pursue God-honoring change.

Outside of our homes, work or school is where we spend the most time and energy. Our occupation or education is usually how we answer the second standard question of social protocol—"What do you do?" Our sense of accomplishment and identity, for better or worse, often emerges from these domains.

▶ **Reflection:** How satisfied are you with your current vocation and/or educational pursuits?

If you experience significant uncertainty and dissatisfaction with life due to your work or selecting the schooling that would help you gain a satisfying career, the resources listed below may be helpful. These works can aid you in discerning how to connect your vocation with God's general call to advance his kingdom in a way that is purposeful and satisfying.

- Timothy Keller, *Every Good Endeavor: Connecting Your Work to God's Work*
- James Petty, *Step by Step: Divine Guidance for Ordinary Christians* (an excellent book on the decision-making process)

Activities Outside the Home

Activities can become triggers for various temptations and insecurities. The weight that we place on our performance can become so significant that it becomes a reason to act out. Our ability to excel at a hobby, beyond how well we succeed at day-to-day life, makes the compliments we receive enticing and can leave us dissatisfied with someone like a spouse, who relies on us for less exciting day-to-day activities. How we perform in a sporting event, on an exam, at a task at work, or in front of a particular group of people can easily become too central, forming our sense of identity and emotional equilibrium.

> ▶ **Reflection:** What activities in your life are important enough to you to disrupt your emotions?

It is easier to understand than live by the simple axiom, "Don't let what you do become the measure of who you are." As we assess the role of activities on our temptation, we want to remember this axiom. In financial negotiations, people are advised to never lose their walkaway power. If they want something so badly that they cannot walk away, they will not get a good deal. Similarly, in emotional regulation, never lose your walkaway power. When a moment becomes so large that you believe your future hangs on it, you will be emotionally crippled and compromised in your response to temptation.

> ▶ **Read Luke 9:23–25 and Matthew 6:33.** God does not want to withhold any good thing from you (Psalm 84:11), but God also does not want you to be owned by any good thing (1 Corinthians 10:23). When an activity becomes the source of your temptation toward sexual sin, it strongly indicates that this line has been

crossed. Your joy will be greater in any activity when you are content in God *without* that activity.

INSPECTION AREA FOUR: *WHAT?*

Entertainment

One of the things we glean from our entertainment preferences is a gauge for what we consider ideal. We entertain ourselves with things like romantic comedies, action movies, sports prowess, beauty, financial opportunities, etc. What we find engaging enough to captivate our attention reveals something significant about us. A problem can emerge when these things move from wholesome to sensual or from enjoyable to what gives meaning to our life. Take inventory of your entertainment choices with the following questions:

- What forms of entertainment are strongly associated with sensuality?
- Which of these do you want to reengage with wise parameters?
- How can you mitigate the risk of relapse?
- Who have you vetted this possibility with?
- Did you become defensive or irritable during the vetting process?

Some entertainment habits are innate sources of sexual temptation. You should avoid these. For instance, don't spend time at sexually themed sports bars to hang out with friends and watch your favorite team. Other sources of entertainment may have become strongly associated with sexual temptation. In another situation, is it wise to attend social gatherings where you are prone to be flirtatious? When you are participating in questionable entertainment, you need to be honest about it and invite scrutiny from those who care about you.

> If you can't bow your head and sincerely thank God for a movie or a symphony or a newscast or a novel—then for you that activity is wrong. Stop arguing with yourself and move on to something else. —Joel Belz[2]

▶ **Reflection:** What does the entertainment you enjoy reveal about the things you value in life? Have these values grown to a point where they are marked by a sense of drivenness, fear, or inadequacy?

Albatross Moments

In "Albatross moments"—occasions that deviate from your regular schedule—your instincts and habits may not be well-suited to the temptations that emerge in these new situations. For instance, vacations are albatross times. We don't have the protections of our normal rhythms and relationships when we're on vacation. That is why albatross moments are often more opportune times that Satan uses to regain a foothold in our life (Luke 4:13). We can't plan for albatross moments, or they wouldn't be albatross moments. But we can think through a response plan for times that catch us by surprise. One such plan follows:

> God does not want to withhold any good thing from you (Psalm 84:11), but God also does not want you to be owned by any good thing (1 Corinthians 10:23).

Remember: What are a few occasions when an unexpected moment resulted in relapse? Use these instances to help you identify the times you are preparing for.

Reflect: What about the moments that you listed above was most disruptive? Use this reflection to learn about yourself. You can't scout the unknown situation, but you can know your response to uncertainty better.

Plan: What are the most important things for you to do when an unforeseen moment of temptation emerges?

SUMMARY OF YOUR HOLISTIC ASSESSMENT

Review your notes from this part of Step 7. You have evaluated many areas of life. It would be easy to be overwhelmed by forty-seven little changes that you think would be good or wise. But that isn't sustainable and becomes impossible to track. Review your notes and look for common themes or overlaps in the kind of changes that would be wise. Become aware of the moments or settings when change is most needed. Focus your attention here.

G4 GROUP DISCUSSION: STEP 7, PART THREE

As you discuss this material in G4 group, these questions are meant to facilitate a more honest and beneficial dialogue about this material. Anyone is free to respond to whichever questions they choose.

Experienced Members

- At this stage your G4 journey, what areas of life are you most focused on refining?
- How was working on the "lower two-thirds of the mountain" more valuable than you expected?

New Members

- Later G4 steps are often a more detailed version of early G4 steps. What have you gleaned from this discussion that is valuable for where you are on your journey?
- What is different in how you heard fellow G4 group members talk about needed changes in their life than how you often feel about needed changes in your own life?
- How can we pray for you?

Everyone

- As you evaluate entertainment (or another area), what wise adaptations do you need to make?
- From the devotion, what is your reaction to the statement, "God does not want to withhold any good thing from you (Psalm 84:11), but God also does not want you to be owned by any good thing (1 Corinthians 10:23)"?
- Have you experienced a significant setback or victory since last meeting that you should tell the group?

STEP 8

PERSEVERE in the new life and identity to which God has called me.

At the end of this step, I want to be able to say . . .

"I can see God's faithfulness over the last [duration of time in G4]. As I have experienced victory, my temptation has changed [describe changes], and my ability to focus on God in non-crisis times has been stretched [examples of growth]. I have come to realize that healthy means more than the absence of sinful behaviors. I am beginning to see more and more of the good things God wants for me [list]. Now that my life includes more than freedom from sin, I am enjoying life so much more."

STEP 8

PART ONE

COMMON LIES AND DISTRACTIONS OPPOSING PERSEVERANCE

The video for this part of Step 8 can be found at: bradhambrick.com/falselove8p1.

As you begin Step 8, you should be enjoying life. Even if you are not there yet, can you identify aspects of your life that make it significantly better than where you've been? Unless you can answer yes to this question and take delight in that answer, perseverance will be grueling. Striving without delighting is exhausting.

One key to persevering is the ability to enjoy an imperfect, in-process life. God does not just delight in you at the culmination of your sanctification. God delights in you right now. He invites you to agree with him—to acknowledge that where he has you in this process is good. This provides the emotional stability and security to persevere.

With that as our starting point, let's ask the question, "What does it look like to continue to follow God from *here*?" You've probably been putting so much energy into getting here that it may not be entirely clear how to prepare yourself for life after G4. What do you do when your life is not focused on fighting sexual sin?

In Step 8 we will look at *post-temptation temptations*—those that uniquely arise when we're doing better. To help you finish strong, we will look at three subjects for this stage in your journey: common lies and distractions to persevering; how progress changes temptation; and preparing for transition from G4.

ENCOUNTERING TYPICAL LIES AND DISTRACTIONS

Strangely, better is not always easier than worse. You likely knew the terrain of your old life better than you know the terrain of your new

life. That is why this section and the next prepare you for how challenges frequently mutate as you leave an old, familiar lifestyle for a
new, unfamiliar one. One of the most effective ways that temptation
mutates is by introducing new lies (or revised versions of old lies) and
distractions. As you read through this section, you should prepare to
listen to yourself. When you hear yourself thinking the following lies,
consider it a warning sign indicating that you
should talk with your support network. The
discussion after each lie (in bold) is intended
to give you truth and perspective to counter
these unhealthy messages.

> One key to
> persevering
> is the ability
> to enjoy an
> imperfect,
> in-process life.

**"I deserve a break. I have been good for a
long time now."** When we talk about taking a
break from our battle with sexual sin, it sounds
very legitimate, but it leads to a return to sin. If
you feel like you need a break, then it is important to make sure you are
living a balanced, sustainable life. "Break" language indicates we feel
like we're sprinting rather than walking out a journey. From the beginning of our journey, we have emphasized a mindset of sustainability.

Often, unrealistic expectations about what you should be doing
fuel our temptation to escape through sin. Too often this same mindset
is applied to efforts like this G4 journey. To persevere, we must pursue
growth at a sustainable pace.

We can set ourselves up for relapse by picturing the perfect life
we think we should be entering. Our unrealistic expectations are the
kryptonite of perseverance as they make us feel justified in taking a
break from what we perceive to be God's expectations. Then we move
toward sin as our relief.

If, however, you assess your expectations and determine they are
realistic but hard, then gaining the strength to endure and enjoy this
lifestyle is what perseverance is all about (Romans 5:3–5; James 1:2–4).
Be sure to ask your support network to verify your assessment and ask
for prayer or encouragement in this process of growth.

- How realistic are your expectations for your time, effort at continued growth, quality of engagement with family, etc.?
- What adjustments need to be made to your expectations to
  make them healthier (either increasing or decreasing)?

"Now I can get back to focusing on what is important to me." This statement can have two connotations. First, it can mean good things that are legitimately important—things like family, work, or personal development. Second, it can mean things that you used to do in excess and which contributed to your sinful lifestyle. The cautions of this section are against this second connotation.

This distraction buys into the notion that overcoming sexual sin is merely about exchanging an unhealthy form of self-focus for more functional forms of self-focus. Times of transition, like Step 8 in your G4 journey, are times when we can inadvertently legitimize sinful self-focus. As innocent as this might appear, we need to realize that sin never remains our servant. Sin introduces itself that way in the beginning—it seems to meet our needs and relieve our stress. Then when we embrace sin, it mutates from servant to master. As you finish this study, several hours per week may be added to your schedule. We noted a similar time vacuum earlier in your G4 journey. Be sure to steward this time productively.

▶ **Reflection:** Review your Step 7 work. What destructive aspects of excessive self-focus do you need to guard against? What God-honoring aspects of using your talents and loving people well do you want to engage more?

▶ **Read Romans 6:12–14.** In these verses, Paul emphasizes the idea that sin desires to reign over us. Sin wants to be our master, to have dominion over our lives. Before we became a Christian we were slaves to sin (v. 20). Salvation removed sin as your master. We were purchased by the blood of Christ (1 Peter 1:19). This G4 journey has been about realizing the freedom that is ours in Christ. We had the right to something we were not experiencing, like an unclaimed inheritance. Now, in Step 8, you are solidifying that freedom by refuting the lies that would lead you back into bondage.

Step 9 will also help you think through the God-honoring aspects of what is important to you. The life God designed you to live will be incredibly satisfying. It will fit you perfectly because it emerges from how God designed you. So do not be concerned that moving on from what *was* important to you will result in a drab life. Allow the improvements in your quality of life from Step 1 to now be confirmation of God's faithfulness from Step 9 and beyond.

"This is not working because temptation is still present. No one else has to work this hard." Only when you stop fighting will temptation become easy—that is, the sense of active resistance will dissipate. But then, as soon as the weight of temptation is removed by succumbing, the greater weights of guilt and consequence are placed on you. Consider this quote from *Mere Christianity*:

> No man knows how bad he is till he has tried very hard to be good. A silly idea is current that good people do not know what temptation means. This is an obvious lie. Only those who try to resist temptation know how strong it is. After all, you find out the strength of the German army by fighting against it, not by giving in. You find out the strength of a wind by trying to walk against it, not by lying down. . . . We never find out the strength of the evil impulse inside us until we try to fight it: and Christ, because He was the only man who never yielded to temptation, is also the only man who knows to the full what temptation means—the only complete realist.
> —C. S. Lewis[1]

Remind yourself that temptation is a sign of having a spiritual life. Only the dulling of one's conscience can remove the sense of temptation in a sin-saturated culture. In a culture of sensuality, we will be perpetually tempted. We will need to live on guard because no one mindlessly drifts toward a God-honoring life.

Resisting temptation can make us tired. But you can now view this fatigue as a sign of growth—like the person whose muscles are tired after lifting weights. What you are experiencing now is the fatigue of maintaining balance in a world that resists balance. That can be seen as a mark of God's grace rather than evidence of being at odds with God's design.

▶ **Reflection:** What remaining moments or types of temptation are discouraging for you? How do these temptations indicate growth and change in your life?

"This is not worth it because [insert desired outcome] is not happening." It is easy to want to be healthy so that [desired outcome occurs]. But how we motivate ourselves is as important as what we accomplish with those motivations. Too often we want freedom from sexual sin for specific outcomes rather than for the inherent value of integrity.

You may have wished for outcomes from this G4 journey that still have not come to fruition. Maybe it's more trust in your marriage or greater freedom from temptation. It is okay to grieve these as disappointments if they are not present yet. But it is important not to allow grief to mutate into bitterness.

You were promised freedom from the power and bondage of sin if you followed Christ. Your life is better for having taken this journey. In a world where we live in the tension of the already and not yet—what the gospel has already accomplished and what has not yet been realized—we often celebrate and grieve at the same time. Allow God to comfort you in the grief over good dreams that have not been realized, and do not throw away the progress you've made.

> ▶ **Reflection:** What good things did you hope for from this G4 journey that have not yet happened?

> ▶ **Reflection:** How are you protecting your heart from discouragement and bitterness? Who is helping you do this?

> ▶ **Read Ezra 3:10–13.** The context is the building of the new temple. Those who had seen the old temple were present, along with those who had not. The first group was crying and the second group was shouting. God had done a good thing in restoring the temple. But the new temple wasn't as grand as the old one. There was a mixed emotional response. Notice that God does not condemn either group of people. It was not wrong to grieve. But God did expect continued faithfulness. Grieving over disappointment was okay, but falling back into the sin pattern of idolatry that resulted in the old temple being destroyed was not okay.

"_____ situation is now more important than pursuing sexual integrity." Rarely would we say this out loud, or even allow ourselves to think it in these words. But this is the lie we believe when we place ourselves back in unwise or compromising situations for practical reasons. Practical becomes a user-friendly synonym for "more important."

> In a world where we live in the tension of the already and not yet—what the gospel has already accomplished and what has not yet been realized—we often celebrate and grieve at the same time.

- "I need to work more hours (get less sleep and spend less time with healthy friends) because I really need to get ahead."
- "I know this form of entertainment is unwholesome, but I don't think it will create those old appetites again."
- "I know it's not wise for me to [one of your Step 6 changes], but I feel like I have to because [excuse]."

When you find yourself trying to alter or relax the changes you made in Steps 6 and 7, recall this lie as a red flag in your mind. This is why it was important for you to document the changes you made throughout this study. It needs to be clear to you when you are undoing the changes that provided freedom.

Those changes were *not* made to help you become strong enough to walk barefoot on enemy turf. Those changes were made because our enemy is stronger than any of us and can only be resisted on the home turf of God's wisdom. Do not fall prey to thinking that victory won under the protection of God's wisdom can persist when we fall back into the arena of worldly wisdom, often called common sense.

The best defense against lies and distractions is to understand the impact of living as if these lies were true. We don't want to be like a college freshman getting their first credit card and believing it's free money. The student needs to understand that using a credit card is spending tomorrow's money today. In Step 8, we've looked at lies and distractions that are equally important to our sexual integrity. Have the courage and maturity to call these lies what they are and avoid living as if they were true.

G4 GROUP DISCUSSION: STEP 8, PART ONE

As you discuss this material in G4 group, these questions are meant to facilitate a more honest and beneficial dialogue about this material. Anyone is free to respond to whichever questions they choose.

Experienced Members

- Which of these lies and distractions is strongest for you right now? What form does it take?
- What did you hope would be true at this point in your journey that isn't yet?

New Members

- Can you see the importance of journaling as you study so that you can look back on commitments you've made?
- Are you encouraged to hear the emphasis on cultivating an enjoyable life as a key part of your G4 journey?
- How can we pray for you?

Everyone

- How does C. S. Lewis's image of walking against the wind help you understand why the middle and later stages of recovery do not get as easy as we often think they should?
- Reflect together on your shared experience of the truth that "sin never remains our servant."
- Have you experienced a significant setback or victory since last meeting that you should tell the group?

STEP 8

PART TWO

HOW PROGRESS CHANGES TEMPTATION

The video for this part of Step 8 can be found at: bradhambrick.com/falselove8p2.

The premise of this part of Step 8 is that temptation changes as we make progress. There are a variety of reasons for this. But the key point is to avoid the assumption that past victory necessitates current victory. That is like the college student who assumes that because they made good grades in high school, excelling in college is a given. New contexts require new skills and new awareness.

Galatians 6:1–5 speaks to both the temptation of those who are "caught in any transgression" and the temptation of those "who are spiritual." Anyone who is in the latter category has spent time in the former; there are no saints who have not and do not struggle with sin. As you have moved from a new member of G4 to an experienced member of the group, you have begun making this transition. Below are four new temptations that emerge as we experience prolonged victory over temptation.

NEW TEMPTATIONS

Disappointment from New Heights

Poverty hurts differently when you've known wealth. As you progress, recurrences of sinful behaviors create a stronger response of guilt and shame than you knew before. We feel like we lost more, that we let more people down, or like we're starting over.

When sexual sin was our "old normal," it was less startling. It can be tempting to allow this intensified guilt from sin in our "new normal" to generate a major sense of failure and to lead us to berate ourselves.

You must recognize intellectually and emotionally that God's grace is sufficient and necessary for any falls into temptation.

A protection from this temptation is to remember that spiritual maturity does not mean independence from God's grace (see next point), but a greater reliance upon it. **Read 1 Timothy 1:12–20.** Notice that toward the end of Paul's ministry he saw himself as more of a sinner, the "chief" of sinners (KJV), than at the beginning (Acts 9). While doubtlessly the offensiveness of Paul's sins decreased from his early sin of murder, he was keenly aware that in his present sinfulness he was in no less need of God's grace than when he was first converted. Paul uses this realization as an encouragement to young Timothy (vv. 18–20) because he realizes the essence of his message is reliance upon grace—the gospel (v. 16).

> ► **Reflection:** How have you responded to disappointments and setbacks with greater despair?

> ► **Reflection:** How have you responded to disappointments and setbacks with greater maturity?

Maturity and Independence

We are often deceived into thinking that spiritual maturity should cause us to be less reliant upon God—so God can focus on the people who are where we used to be, we might think. This is a dangerous mutation in our temptation. It is like a great oak tree thinking its height means it no longer requires the soil. As soon as it detaches from the soil, its height only serves to quicken its fall and increase the damage that is done. The truth is that spiritual maturity can only be expressed as greater dependence upon God.

> ► **Read Galatians 2:18–21.** Notice that Paul warns against rebuilding what was torn down (v. 18). This is exactly what a false view of maturity does—it relies on the Law (or the law we give ourselves) rather than the humility of perpetually acknowledging our God-reliance. With this warning, Paul lays down the principle that maturity is less of me and more of Christ (v. 20). As a caterpillar matures into a butterfly, we are called to mature into something different. We started grounded and crawling in our

independence from God (the essence of sin). We mature into people who realize dependence upon God is freedom, like the butterfly finds freedom allowing its wings to ride a summer breeze. The caterpillar must die to become a butterfly. The butterfly must trust the breeze to fly. As we overcome temptation to sexual sin, we allow the old man to die in order to become who God made us to be and rely on his grace to propel us into the next seasons of life.

Spiritual maturity can only be expressed as greater dependence upon God.

▶ **Reflection:** How are you beginning to see maturity as being synonymous with greater dependence on God?

Pressure of New Opportunities

With growth comes opportunity, and not necessarily because we are seeking it. Managing your life well almost inevitably brings more opportunities into your life and more opportunities to aid others as well. We may be excited or intimidated by the opportunities that begin to come our way. But we can be sure that with maturity will come opportunities to offer others the same hope we have received (2 Corinthians 1:3–5).

▶ **Exercise:** Keep a list of new responsibilities and opportunities that God brings into your life as you progress in your G4 journey.

Give thanks for these opportunities. Remember they are tokens of God's grace, not burdens. When they feel heavy, ask for help and talk about this weight with a friend. Blessings can be heavy, but they only become burdens when we hide the uncertainty or insecurity we feel. This is a mark of maturity as we humbly depend on God and his people.

Remember that merely gaining freedom from sexual sin is not the end of your journey. Sin was sapping your energy to do things God called you to do, stealing the time in which you would do them, and undermining the confidence that God would bless your efforts. Be discerning about not overloading on these opportunities. But realize that these opportunities to care for others are a significant part of becoming the person God created you to be (Matthew 22:37–40).

Having Answers Instead of Questions

As you mature and receive new opportunities, you will likely be looked to for more answers. Your responses to the challenges of life are becoming grounded and hopeful, so people will want to know how you would approach their challenges. You begin to get the privilege of joining people at earlier stages in their G4 journey.

> Remember that merely gaining freedom from sexual sin is not the end of your journey.

This is a time when pride can return in more subtle and socially acceptable ways. We must never think that because a question is brought to us that we are the source of its answer. We must never mistake the glory of the answer for the glory of the vessel that has been entrusted to carry that answer (2 Corinthians 4:7–18). We are merely the conduit of the hope and perspective that we have received from God and others in our journey.

▶ **Exercise:** Use the notes you've taken on your G4 journey to root the hope and perspective you offer others in the biblical truths that have undergirded your G4 journey.

▶ **Read James 3:1–12.** Notice that James is writing to Christians coming out of the struggle of dispersion by religious persecution (see James 1:1). Some are now rising to the position of teacher (3:1), and he warns those about the temptation that comes with the increased power of their words in this new role. The message is that the awesome power of influence—given in the imagery of bridles and fire—should keep us humble as we are coming into new positions of influence.

The changes we've discussed in this part of Step 8 are things we should be both excited about and cautious toward. We should be excited because they are indicators of God's grace at work in our life producing growth. They are signs of maturation and progress. We should be cautious because they reveal the transition into new unfamiliar roles. Give yourself the freedom to be both excited and humbled at the same time.

G4 GROUP DISCUSSION: STEP 8, PART TWO

As you discuss this material in G4 group, these questions are meant to facilitate a more honest and beneficial dialogue about this material. Anyone is free to respond to whichever questions they choose.

Experienced Members

- How have/did you see temptation change for you as you entered Steps 7 and 8?
- What was the same—and what needed to change—in how you faced these temptations?

New Members

- Does it encourage or discourage you to think about temptation mutating as you progress?
- How does seeing the emphasis on dependence later in the G4 journey help curb your instinct toward independence early in your recovery process?
- How can we pray for you?

Everyone

- Which of these four changes in temptation are most prevalent in your life and emotions?
- From the devotion on Galatians 2, what changes are you most prone to rebuild after tearing them down?
- Have you experienced a significant setback or victory since last meeting that you should tell the group?

STEP 8

PART THREE

PREPARING FOR TRANSITION FROM G4

The video for this part of Step 8 can be found at: bradhambrick.com/falselove8p3.

This third part of Step 8 may feel like a change of pace. That is because it no longer has overcoming temptation as its primary focus. Instead, this section asks, "What should my life begin to look like next—that is, after G4?" Again, we don't overcome sin for the sake of overcoming sin. We overcome sin to live the life that God intended. This part of Step 8 is about laying the foundation to live wisely in your new freedom.

PREPARING FOR LIFE AFTER G4

Make Sure You Are in a Small Group

Trust takes time. If you have been going through this material in a G4 group, the baton of trust will soon be passed to relationships less focused on recovery. One-way helping relationships are not healthy long-term relationships as your primary source of support and encouragement. For a season or as a supplement to authentic peer-based friendships, these can be great. But for the long-term, we need to learn to be honest with and gain support from reciprocal friendships. You also want to expand the focus of your spiritual maturity from just overcoming sexual sin to the full spectrum of character formation and discipleship.

> We don't overcome sin for the sake of overcoming sin. We overcome sin to live the life that God intended.

Small groups are the primary location for this to occur. The name of these groups may vary from church to church: Sunday school, community groups, missional communities, etc. The point is that you need to participate in one in ways that are commensurate with how you've participated in G4. Talk with your pastor if you need help identifying which small group would be a good fit for you.

Some people object, "But these groups are shallower than G4. People in these groups aren't as serious about making significant changes in their life." That may be true. But that is why we say *the church needs G4, and G4 needs the church.*

- *The church needs G4* because there is great benefit to have subject-specific communities that are intensely focused on areas of needed change. It is hard for the general discipleship ministry of a church to do what G4 does. But the church also needs the model of G4's intentionality and vulnerability in its discipleship ministries to provide examples of what it looks like to do in-depth sanctification work in highly authentic relationships.
- *G4 needs the church* because we need to avoid having our struggle become our identity and reducing our spiritual maturity to how we're doing with a single struggle. You are more than your struggle with sexual sin. While God may have you remain in G4 as a leader, God intends to use you in ways that are outside G4. Things God wants to do in and through you are meant to be done in concert with your local church.

We emphasize becoming part of a small group now so that you don't graduate from G4 without being established in a community. Your remaining time in Steps 8 and 9 should include meaningful engagement with a small group. This community will fulfill the roles we are about to discuss.

Learn Accountability and Encouragement on a Broader Scale

Walking through this material with your G4 group may be the first time you have experienced ongoing, Christian accountability and encouragement. Accountability is not just for life-dominating struggles. It is part of God's definition of "healthy." People who do not have relationships that include honesty about their struggles, as well as accountability and encouragement to help them with those struggles, are people who are becoming unhealthy.

As you move from G4 to a general small group, you may wonder what accountability and encouragement will look like now. The seven points below are meant to guide you in the kind of relationships you are looking to form with your small group:

1. **Voluntary.** Accountability is not something you have; it is something you do. You must disclose what needs to be known to benefit from relationships. Hopefully, the experience you have had in G4 will encourage you to remain transparent and vulnerable.

2. **Trusted.** The other person is someone you trust, admire their character, and believe has good judgment. You are encouraged to join a small group now so that you can build this trust before graduating from G4.

3. **Mutual.** Relationships that are one-sided tend to be short-lived. In the small group, you will hear the weaknesses and struggles of others as you share your own. You will help carry their burdens as they help carry yours (Galatians 6:1–2).

4. **Scheduled.** Accountability that is not scheduled tends to fade. This is why small groups that meet on a weekly basis are an ideal place for accountability to occur. Everyone knows when to meet and has a shared expectation for how the accountability conversations will begin.

5. **Relational.** We want spiritual growth to become a lifestyle, not an event. This means that we invite accountability to be a part of our regular conversations, not just something that we do at a weekly meeting. There should be times when we are doing accountability and don't realize it; we're just being honest about what's hard.

6. **Comprehensive.** Accountability that exclusively fixates on one subject tends to become repetitive and fade. It also tends to reduce success to trusting God in a single area of life. Good accountability calls us to become more like Christ in every facet of our life.

7. **Encouraging.** Too often the word *accountability* carries the connotation of a sin hunt. When that is the case, accountability is only perceived to be working when it is negative. However, accountability that lasts should celebrate growth in character as fervently as it works on slips in character.

If you are looking for a tool to help develop these kinds of relationships in a small group that avoids making a discipleship environment overly therapeutic, consider reading *Transformative Friendships: 7 Questions to Deepen Any Relationship* (Brad Hambrick) in this Church-Based Counseling series.[1]

You are more than your struggle with sexual sin.

Have a Plan for Future Study

A general rule of life is, we walk forward, but we drift backward. This G4 curriculum has provided intentional, structured processes for you to follow. If you leave that structure without a plan for continued growth, you will likely regress. Ephesians 5:15–16 calls us to live intentionally, recognizing that time minus direction equals decay, not growth.

This entire study has been filled with devotional Bible studies. If you have not been taking the time to read the passages and reflect on the commentary and questions that accompany them, consider using those as a guide for daily Bible reading. This will be a way to reinforce your G4 journey and further solidify the biblical basis for what you've learned.

Step 7 in this curriculum referenced many resources that might be beneficial for you. If one of them stood out as significant, begin reading it as you complete Step 8 and begin forming a relationship of trust with a small group at your church. If none of these resources seems like a good fit, then consider studying Michael Emlet's *Saints, Sufferers, and Sinners* as a resource to help you solidify your progress.[2]

Make a Formal Transition Plan

As you prepare to graduate from G4, use the following checklist to write out your transition plan:

- List the relationships and practices that need to be in place before you graduate.
- Consider any imminent, upcoming life events that would be better to navigate with the support of your G4 group.
- Write out a concise summary of the key truths and changes that have been most influential from your G4 journey. Share these with your small group.
- Write out your yellow flags (don't wait for the red ones) that are warning signs of relapse. Also, share these with your small group.

Review your plan with your G4 group. Get their input on what needs to be added to the plan. The graduation of a group member is an important event in the life of every member in the group. Honor the significance of your pending graduation by giving weight to the encouragement and concerns raised by your fellow G4 members.

Perseverance is boring and exciting at the same time. It is boring because change usually does not happen as fast in this phase. Change was bold and obvious early in recovery. But change that is fast is often not as solid—it's more like a weed than a tree. Boring growth is solid growth. This is not meant to be pejorative. Satisfying growth is not boring, but it takes time. When you look back over a stretch of months or a year and can say both "Not much has changed" and also "Life is good," that is a momentous testimony to God's faithfulness and your perseverance. As that becomes your testimony, you are ready to enter Step 9.

▶ **Read Isaiah 61:1–4.** Notice that this passage celebrates people who are "oaks of righteousness" (v. 3). Oaks are strong trees that grow slowly. That is what you've done to arrive at Step 8 in G4. You've set aside the necessary time to allow your growth to become solid and strong. Then notice that these oaks of righteousness are people who have grown during trials and have had their tears wiped away. God intended to use these oaks to build up the ancient ruins and repair the cities (v. 4), in the same way that through your time at G4 God has rebuilt your life and given you a testimony that can help others. Finally, notice that the oaks were captives set free (v. 1) and that they received "the oil of gladness" (v. 3)—all so that the Lord may be glorified (v. 3). Much like the oaks, you have been set free to glorify God. And your work to cultivate a fruitful life from what sexual sin destroyed will continue long after you graduate from G4.

G4 GROUP DISCUSSION: STEP 8, PART THREE

As you discuss this material in G4 group, these questions are meant to facilitate a more honest and beneficial dialogue about this material. Anyone is free to respond to whichever questions they choose.

Experienced Members

- How has your time in G4 enriched your Christian relationships outside G4?
- What have you learned from seeing other members graduate from G4?

New Members

- What encouragement do you take from the fact that G4 is designed for you to graduate from it?
- Even earlier in your G4 journey, how are you challenged by the idea, "we walk forward, but we drift backward"?
- How can we pray for you?

Everyone

- In your own words, summarize what is meant by "The church needs G4, and G4 needs the church."
- In your own words, summarize what is meant by "Perseverance is boring and exciting at the same time."
- Have you experienced a significant setback or victory since last meeting that you should tell the group?

STEP 9
STEWARD all of my life
for God's glory.

At the end of this step, I want to be able to say . . .

**"God has been faithful in my battle against sin.
I am learning what it means to live out of my
new identity in Christ. God's faithfulness has pushed
me to ask the question, 'How can I be a conduit
of his grace to others?' As I have sought God,
examined my life, and consulted with fellow
believers, I believe this is what it looks like for me
to steward God's grace now [describe]."**

STEP 9
PART ONE

NINE QUESTIONS TO STEWARD YOUR LIFE FOR GOD'S GLORY

The video for this part of Step 9 can be found at: bradhambrick.com/falselove9p1.

I f the law of God can be summarized in a positive command (Matthew 22:37–40), then we must end this study talking about how to run to God rather than merely how to run from sin. Life is not about what we avoid, but what we pursue. How we run to God's design for our life finds a unique expression in each person's life. For this reason, you will do most of the writing in this step. We will simply provide you with the questions to consider.

The goal is to find things that you could give yourself to more passionately than you once gave yourself to your sin. Not just temporal, slightly healthier things, but eternally significant things that create a sense of purpose and keep you connected with a community of faith as you continue to grow toward Christlikeness.

> ▶ **Read Luke 11:24–26.** This is a terrifying warning about removing sin without also replacing it with God's purposes for your life. If we replace sin with the contradiction of a "God-ignoring healthy life," we become proud and defensive regarding further change. Our idols (Step 3) become more functional, so the warning system of adverse consequences is muted. Then, when our idols cease to satisfy and become disruptive again (as they inevitably will), we are less likely to return to God, the Bible, and the gospel because they didn't really free us the first time. Indeed, "the last state of that person is worse than the first" (v. 26). This is why Step 9 is essential for ongoing victory over sin.

▶ **Read Ephesians 2:8–10.** In G4, we have examined the scope of the gospel (vv. 8–9) and the good works that come as we live out the gospel (v. 10). The nine steps are merely the gospel in slow motion. We are not now exiting the gospel to do good works, but instead cultivating the fruit of the gospel. It's all still grace—we're not to continue by our own effort (Titus 2:11–12). Paul says God has prepared good works for every believer and these should define our daily lives because we "should walk in them" (v. 10). This will give you hope for answers to the questions you will be asked in Step 9. You can have confidence from the promises of Scripture that God has a design for your life and wants you to know that design.

> Life is not about what we avoid, but what we pursue.

GRADUATE G4 WITH PURPOSE AND ON MISSION

As you read through and answer these nine questions, remember God's patience and timing. You will be able to engage immediately some aspects of God's design. But you will also want to serve God in ways that require you to be more mature or equipped before you are prepared to fulfill them. The most important thing is beginning to have a vision for life that involves being God's servant and actively engaging that vision where you are currently able.

1. **Am I willing to commit my life to whatever God asks of me?** This is a "do not pass go" question. If you are unwilling to commit your life to God, the answers you give to each subsequent question will be biased. Do not get lost in guilt or pretend that your answer is yes (both responses would lead you back into an addictive lifestyle). Rather, identify the obstacle. What cost are you unwilling to pay? Put it into words. Wrestle with what it means to trust God with this part of your life.

   Are there specific things you believe God is asking of you? Be sure to record your thoughts on this question before reflecting on the subsequent questions.

2. **What roles have I neglected that God has placed me in?** The first part of being a good steward of one's life is to fulfill one's primary

roles with excellence. When Paul says in Ephesians 5:17 that we are to "understand what the will of the Lord is," he goes on in 5:22–6:9 to describe God's design for major life roles (spouse, parent, child, employee, and employer).

3. **What are my spiritual gifts?** Stewarding your life for the glory of God involves utilizing the spiritual gifts God has given you. God gives spiritual gifts that coincide with the calling he places on every believer's life. Read Romans 12:1–8 and 1 Corinthians 12:1–30. If you need further assistance discerning this, talk to a pastor about taking a spiritual gifts inventory.

4. **What group of people (age, struggle, career, ethnicity, etc.) am I burdened to help?** From God's earliest covenant with people, his intention was to bless us that we might be a blessing to others (Genesis 12:2). Investing your life in those you have a burden for allows you to be other-minded and find joy in it.

5. **What am I passionate about?** At this point in the stewardship evaluation, you can begin to see Psalm 37:3–8 fulfilled in your life. Do I delight in the Lord? What are the God-exalting "desires" in your life (v. 4)? What wholesome activities can you give yourself to and feel more energized afterward than before you started?

6. **With what talents or abilities has God blessed me?** These don't have to be spiritual gifts. Read the amazing description of abilities God gave Bezalel and how he used those abilities to serve God (Exodus 31:1–11). Think through the skills and expertise you have accumulated in your life to evaluate your abilities.

7. **What are my unique life experiences?** Both pleasant and unpleasant experiences should be listed here. We are sometimes tempted to think that God can only use the good or the spiritual experiences of our lives. God is glad to use our successes (Matthew 5:16), but God also delights in displaying his grace by transforming our low points for his glory (2 Corinthians 1:3–5).

8. **Where do my talents and passions match with the needs in my church and community?** We should seek to steward our lives

in cooperation with our local church. God's way of blessing and maturing those we serve is through the body of Christ, the church. By identifying where your gifts, burdens, passions, and abilities fit within (or expand) your church's ministries, you are maximizing the impact of that service on those you are seeking to bless.

9. **How would God have me bring these things together to glorify him?** This is not a new question, but a summary question. Look back over what you have written. Talk about it with your Christian friends, family, mentor, or pastors. Dedicate a time to prayerfully ask God for a sense of direction. Then begin serving to steward your life for God's glory.

"Blessed are those who hunger and thirst for righteousness, for they shall be satisfied."—Matthew 5:6

G4 GROUP DISCUSSION: STEP 9, PART ONE

As you discuss this material in G4 group, these questions are meant to facilitate a more honest and beneficial dialogue about this material. Anyone is free to respond to whichever questions they choose.

Experienced Members

- As you reflected on these questions, what do you believe is God's purpose for you in this next season of life?
- Which of these questions was most influential for you in discerning what God has for you next?

New Members

- Does talking about Step 9 create a sense of wanting to rush your journey?
- How does seeing the culmination of your G4 journey create hope and motivation for you?
- How can we pray for you?

Everyone

- Can you review the nine steps and articulate how they are merely the gospel in slow motion? Could you share the gospel with a friend as you told them your story of walking this nine-step journey?

- Based on the devotional from Luke 11, what cautions do you take for your journey?
- Have you experienced a significant setback or victory since last meeting that you should tell the group?

APPENDIX A

A Word to G4 Group Leaders

Thank you for your willingness to lead a G4 group! This postscript is a microcosm of *Facilitating Church-Based Counseling Groups: A Leader's Guide for Group-Based Counseling Ministry* (New Growth, 2023), the leader's guide for G4 series books. The points below are explained and illustrated in greater detail in that resource. If you have already read *Facilitating*, this postscript is your cheat sheet reminder page. If you have not yet read *Facilitating*, then this is your sampler's platter to entice you to take the next step in training as a counseling group leader.

Here are a few things you need to know about leading a G4 group:

- G4 series curriculums facilitate an **open group model**—meaning anyone can join the group at any time and everyone present is likely to be at a different place on their journey.
- Because G4 is an open group model, your role is *not* to serve as a counselor for each person in the group; instead, you are a **facilitator of the group**.
- As the group facilitator, your two primary tasks are to **lead the discussion** each evening and **manage the morale** of the group.
- The **video teaching** for each segment of this journey is meant to alleviate the pressure for you to feel like a subject matter expert. For this curriculum, the video teaching can be found at **bradhambrick.com/falselove**. The QR code at the beginning of each new section will take participants to the video clip for that section.
- The **expectation for each participant** of the group is to (a) faithfully attend G4, (b) watch the video clip for the section

they are working on, (c) read, reflect, and complete exercises for that section, and (d) come ready to discuss the progress or challenges they faced that week. Since everyone works at their own pace, you're not assessing the pace of their journey, simply that they are still committed to moving forward.

- Counseling groups like G4 are for those who are **ready to change** or strongly considering their need for change. It is not your role or the role of the group to convince people to take steps they are unwilling to take. The group exists to support, not convince.

- Each **G4 curriculum is intentionally long.** No one should finish nine steps in nine weeks. While that might give you a good education about sexual addiction, it is not sufficient time to cement change over a life-dominating struggle. In reality, you may not finish one part of each step each week. G4 is less about education (mastering content) and more about transformation (accomplishing change). That takes time. G4 is not a race. No prizes are given for finishing first or fast. The reward of a restored life is the fruit of finishing well.

- As you can begin to see, G4 is a **place of support with a curriculum that provides guidance**. As you think of G4, those should be your two guiding principles. First, lead the group in a way that it becomes a place of mutual support. Second, allow the curriculum to provide counsel. These two components come together in the group sharing time as members hear stories of how the curriculum was applied in each other's lives.

- When **someone needs more help than G4 can provide**, aid them in finding a resource in your community that provides that care while continuing (if they are willing) to provide the support of your G4 group. You are not failing if someone needs more guidance than your G4 group can provide. Do what you can do well, and point people to additional resources as needed. In most cases, those additional resources will be more effective because of the support of G4. You will notice that there are not a lot of stories in G4 curriculum. That is because the testimonies of fellow G4 participants are the most powerful illustrations.

- To accomplish these objectives, we **recommend a schedule for a G4 group** that follows the outline below. Each segment is defined and illustrated in greater depth in *Facilitating Church-Based Counseling Groups.*
  - » Welcome and orient new guests.
  - » Personal updates (5–10 minutes).
  - » Facilitating and sharing (30–40 minutes). These are often done simultaneously or in either order. You are free to lead your group in the way that serves it best.
    - Covering a step or step segment (10–15 minutes).
    - Personal step work progress and accountability (20–25 minutes).
  - » Prayer (5–10 minutes).

Serve your group with these general parameters in mind. Don't underestimate the value of having a weekly place to meet, discuss, and receive encouragement for a shared life struggle. Life-dominating struggles make us feel alone, like no one else could understand. Your group is an oasis that dispels this lie. As the leader, you hold out hope that, while we may not see the change we desire week-to-week, when we look at the lives of faithful participants from month-to-month, we are encouraged by God's faithfulness. As we look at the legacy of a group year-to-year, we move from encouragement to amazement at what God accomplishes.

G4 is a long-game ministry. Stay the course, be faithful in your role, encourage participants to persevere in the process, and you will see lives transformed by the gospel in ways that sustain your soul in this weighty ministry!

APPENDIX B

How to Talk to Children When Sexual Sin Affects the Family

W hen sexual sin comes to light in a family, every member of that family is impacted. Not only is the impact *broad*, but the impact is also *unique* in how it affects each family member. The most innocent, and the ones who frequently received the least quality or quantity of care, are the children.

Children of all ages need both *honesty* and *hope* amid the disruption that inevitably ensues. The facts, which should be age-appropriately honest, need to be delivered clearly but with as much hope as the situation allows. As parents (both offended and offending parent), our instinct is to shield our children from this hurtful reality and to try to make things "less painful" for them.

"Less painful" is an appropriate goal if it does not come at the cost of being truthful, creating unrealistic expectations, or avoiding legitimate questions of a child. If "less painful" compromises the child's age-appropriate ability to know the truth or ability to anticipate the future (at least to the degree that is possible), then "less painful" produces more harm than benefit.

CASE STUDY

The following case study is a fictitious example of a family of six walking through the process of a mother slowly finding out that her husband is committing adultery with a coworker. A family of six was depicted as a teaching tool to represent more ages of children and desirable responses. It is meant to help you apply the recommendations that follow by providing an example that is less personal than your current situation.

> Caitlyn is three years old. She stays home with her mom most days, enjoys being outside, and loves reading stories with her dad. She has older siblings who attend school. Caleb is six and in the first grade, Kayla is eleven and just entering middle school, while Jacob is fourteen and starting high school. From the outside, all looks good for this family.
>
> The family is active at church. The children are involved in sports, drama, and other extracurricular activities. Dad works hard to support the family financially. They look like your typical American family, the kind that you would want to have over for dinner. But behind closed doors things are quite different. Dad is critical and emotionally absent much of the time. He will do what is asked, but he rarely seems excited and does not initiate family time or individual activities with the children. He asks the standard questions about grades, school, and friends, but he seems uninterested beyond these surface-level engagements.
>
> Mom does her best to compensate for Dad's lack of involvement by over-involvement. She tries to make sure the kids have everything they need and want. This creates tension between Mom and Dad because they can never get ahead financially. For this and other reasons, neither values time with the other.
>
> The most recent tension appeared after Mom found some emails Dad had sent to a coworker. The emails seemed flirtatious and inappropriate. Dad quickly minimized them and proceeded to berate Mom for looking at his personal activities and not trusting him.
>
> Over the course of the next few months, Mom continued to see emails and eventually text messages that confirmed her suspicion that Dad was having an affair. After multiple attempts at confrontation and many arguments, Dad admitted his actions. Mom was devastated, Dad was angry, *and the children were confused.*

WHAT DOES THE FAMILY DO NOW?

The scenario above is meant to serve as a framework for caring for children when a parent's sexual sin impacts their family. There are many things to keep in mind as you prepare for this type of conversation. The points below are meant to orient you to how these situations affect a child, the appropriate expectations of a child when they first learn of the sexual sin, the expectations after learning of the sexual sin, and the type of assistance a child needs to process this information.

- An event of this magnitude and the subsequent parental conflict, absence, and distraction can be severely disruptive for children, even adult children outside the home.
- If your child has not yet reached puberty or has no knowledge of or exposure to sex, your conversations about what has happened should *not* describe what happened in sexual language.
- As children age and develop, which includes their social development and sexual awareness, they may ask questions about things that have happened during this time. Answering these questions in age-appropriate ways is an important part of helping them process their grief.
- Your child's feelings may be more intense or less intense than the feelings of the offended spouse. Both parents need to accept whatever feelings surface, help the child to name those feelings, and understand how those feelings relate to the changes in their life, home, and family.
- If an experience of this magnitude happens to children who are preschool age or older, they will remember it and may need to process those memories at later developmental stages as they are able to fully comprehend more of their personal family history.
- Most children will not process their emotions about an event of this magnitude (that is, healthily assimilate these events into their life story) until they feel safe enough to do it. Once you and your spouse have reached a better place and feel as if you are moving on, may be when the children begin to process their feelings. This will feel like it drags out the healing process for the parents, but you cannot rush your children through their

process any more than the offending spouse could be rushed to repentance or the offended spouse rushed to forgiveness.

- The biggest damage that has been done is undermining the child's sense of security at home and definition of love. This is true regardless of the age of the child. The initial care and after-care for a child should focus upon providing a healthy sense of security and balanced expression of love.

- When it comes to having the "what's going on" talk, the ideal situation would be for both parents and potentially a neutral, trusted third person to talk to the children together (especially if one or both parents are likely to become emotionally disrupted during the conversation).

- The content of the "what's going on" talk should be decided before talking to the child. If an agreement cannot be reached, wait until an agreement can be reached. The delay should be as short as possible because the longer you wait, the more confusing the resulting changes become for the children.

- There may need to be more than one conversation, depending on the age differences of your children. If your children are in the same developmental range, one conversation with all family members present will suffice. If your children are at different ages and developmental stages, do not try to talk to everyone at the same time. But do make sure that what you say to everyone is as consistent in content as age-appropriateness will allow. Older children should be told if there are things their younger siblings do not know and do not need to know at the current time.

- Make sure someone in your children's lives will be their support. This is especially important for the older children and even children who are out of the house and often get overlooked in this process.

- If the sexual sin will not result in lifestyle changes (parental separation, divorce, job loss, pregnancy, etc.), seek counsel about what to disclose to your children. Your children may only need to know that you and your spouse have encountered problems because of hurtful choices by a parent and you both are trying to make things better.

- Encourage children to ask questions as they have them. It is unreasonable and unhealthy to expect children to formulate their questions at the "information meeting." When you give them the freedom to ask questions, it is wise to also tell them you don't have all the answers and that there may be some things that will stay between Mom and Dad. Remember that children process at a slower pace and may ask questions well after this initial conversation. Being prepared for this prevents the emotional processing of your children from setting you back emotionally. A negative emotional response by the parents to a child's question often reinforces the common false belief that the child has some responsibility for what happened in the marriage.

- Guard yourself from feeling the need to "make up" for what is happening in your family. Neither gifts nor penance will make up for the offense or alleviate its impact. If anything, they will teach a distorted view of the gospel, repentance, forgiveness, reconciliation, and family. Patiently submitting to the reconciliation process (when possible) is the most helpful thing for your children. Only God can heal the hurt in your children, not imbalanced love.

GUIDANCE FOR CONVERSATIONS BY AGE

If the sexual sin will result in a lifestyle change—parental separation, divorce, job loss, pregnancy, etc.—you will need to have discussions with the children. We will consider each stage of development, but all the previous material should be considered relevant, unless something said about the next maturation level contradicts the earlier material. Therefore, regardless of your children's ages, please read all the sections below.

Birth Through Five Years

While you may think that children at these ages are unable to tell something is going on, children are very perceptive at reading their environment. If Mom is frequently crying, Dad is angry, or there is bickering and fighting, even young children can tell. They may become more "needy," experience developmental delays, or regress in already learned skills as expressions of how changes in the home environment are affecting them.

The goal for parents is to be both authentic and reassuring. (Faking calm only when you think the child is looking reveals that their parents are not being honest.) You may be defensive about your sin being known. But you are still a parent. You cannot be silent, brooding, defensive, or blame-shifting without impacting your children. If restraining these responses is hard for you, ask for help. Take time to see a counselor or ask a friend to work through *False Love* with you.

Don't have conversations with your preschooler unless a decision is made for the offending spouse to leave for an extended or indefinite period. If spouses are staying together and no one is moving out, preschool children do not need to know what has happened. Later, when they are adults or older teens, there may be a time when it's beneficial to share what God has done or what happened. But preschool children have no way of comprehending what you would tell them. The main goal at this age is to provide consistency, love, and safety—to fulfill their greatest needs. Lean on friends and trusted caregivers during this time.

If the offending parent leaves the house and the child is between two and five years old, you should give some explanation as to where the parent is going. The optimal plan would be for this conversation to be factual and done together or potentially with a neutral, trusted third person present (especially if one or both parents are likely to become emotionally disrupted during the conversation). The person leaving should be the primary speaker and communicate the following information:

> I am going to stay with (location—the child will need to know because it can cause more anxiety to say he or she is just going away) for (duration—it is important to tell the child the duration so they know an ending point. If a duration cannot be determined, then be honest and tell them you don't know how long). I know it will be hard for you to be away from me, so I will come to see you (give visitation plan).

Notice in this conversation that you did not give the preschooler the answer to the why question. Most will ask, but some may not. Do not try to answer the why question for preschoolers unless they ask because it is hard for them to spontaneously transition to abstract thinking, especially in an emotionally powerful setting.

If they ask why, the offending parent should tell them the following:

> I made some choices that I should not have made. These things really hurt Mommy/Daddy. Sometimes, if we really hurt someone, we need to give them time and space. So I am going to (location) to give Mommy/Daddy some space. [Reiterate your love for them and that you will miss them.]

There will be tears, shock, and an inability to comprehend what you are saying. Children's brains are not developed for this type of transition. They do not have the life experience to grasp what it means or know what to do when a parent is absent for punitive reasons ("punishment" is the category they have for comprehending a marriage time-out). Be patient. Prepare for tantrums and disruptions to their sleeping and eating patterns.

The experience of children (at any of the ages discussed) will look a lot like grief because they are grieving the loss of what they have known as "normal." Thinking of their response as grief rather than defiance will help you comfort them.

If the parents stay together, it is important to keep a preschooler's routine as normal as possible. Enrolling in programs like Parent's Day Out or preschool for a couple of days per week may allow the offended parents time to work through what has happened.

As a parent, the offended spouse bears the role of modeling how to respond to these types of hurts. This includes encouraging the child to express their feelings and telling the offending parent what they are thinking. You are not responsible for the other parent's behavior, but you can teach your child during this difficult time how to handle conflict and express emotions healthily. It is important to think about what you are teaching your child through your modeling. Children will learn more about emotions, reconciliation, and relationships from what you see you do than what you "teach" them during this time.

Elementary-Age Children

Elementary-age children are more verbal and have more cognitive ability than preschoolers, but they should not have sexual knowledge or understanding yet. When talking with your elementary-aged child about what has happened, it is wise to say things like:

"Mom/Dad made choices that hurt me."
"Mom and Dad are working on making our marriage better."
"Mom/Dad is working on forgiving . . ."
"Mom/Dad is working on building trust with . . ."

Children at this age will ask lots of questions. They may ask "What did you do?" "Are you getting divorced?" "Do you still love Mom/Dad?" Be honest where you can, but when the answer to their question is not age appropriate or is undecided, it is appropriate to say, "Some of what happens between Mom and Dad is not helpful for you to know," or "We are still deciding about that."

Reassurance of your love for them is important during and after each of these conversations. It is beneficial to point them toward God and prayer. Pray with your child after these conversations, but pray in ways that express where they are at. Don't try to teach them what to think or how to respond as you talk to God. Teaching with our eyes closed isn't really praying. Listen to your child and allow your prayer to model how to express their feelings to God.

These conversations are an opportunity to talk about how even parents let them down, but God is faithful and will not let them down. If the offending spouse decides to leave the home for a time, then it will be necessary to have a conversation much like you had with your two- to five-year-old.

Middle / High School Children

Middle school and high school children are becoming sexually aware. By this age most parents have had "the talk" explaining sex. If this is the case, then being factually honest about sexual sin is appropriate. You would rather your child hear your confession about what happened than learn about it from someone else.

If the sin is adultery or an emotional affair, you should not give details about the sexual relationship. It is easy, when hurt and angry, to be more vivid or derogatory than is necessary. There is no social or redemptive value in a child having that information. However, it is important to share information that allows them to understand their family story and navigate their social world.

Children in these age categories will likely be thinking about how this affects their life. Teens are still at an egocentric stage of development, so a primary fear for them often centers on how their life will be altered. One tendency for teens will be to take the role of protector for the offended spouse. This is an understandable but unhealthy role for a teenager. While it is natural for there to be a loss of trust with the offending parent, an emerging "us" (teen and offended parent) versus "them" (offending parent) makes it harder to maintain a healthy parent-child relationship in the years before the child becomes an independent adult.

> Listen to your child and allow your prayer to model how to express their feelings to God.

Another frequent dynamic is for the teen to defend or excuse the actions of the offending parent as an expression of their desire for things to get back to normal. The offended parent needs to be careful not to be defensive or condemning of their teenager's compassion. Neither should the offending parent leverage this compassion to form an alliance with that child. Both parents should affirm that this is a hard situation with few win-win choices as the parents work to determine the future of the marriage and family. Give the teen time and space to continue processing their own feelings, ask if they have questions, and provide the freedom to appropriately share the emotions they are experiencing.

Adult Children

Sometimes children who have moved out of the house are thought to be unaffected. This is not true. Children, regardless of their age, will feel like their basis of security is shaken when their parents' marriage is traumatized or dissolved. Adult children may feel like everything they knew growing up was false. They will question whether the offending parent was really who they thought they were. Disclosure of sexual sin can be used as an excuse to turn from God and how they were raised.

It is immensely valuable for adult children to have an adult who knows them and is aware of the situation reach out and check on them regularly. Unless someone reaches out to them, they are forced to process things alone and without the benefit of seeing what their parents are going through. An objective opinion, not just what their mom and dad are saying, will be important for them to process these changes in their home of origin.

WHEN A CHILD FINDS OUT FIRST

What do you do if your child comes to you because they saw a parent looking at things on the internet or flirting with someone in public? In this situation, it is important for the offended spouse to assure the child of the following things:

- They did the right thing by coming to you. Continue to validate that they did the right thing in speaking up, that they are not in trouble, and that they did not get anyone else in trouble (witnesses don't cause problems; they only observe them).
- You will do your best to find out what happened. Once you do have an answer, plan a time for both parents to talk with the children.

If a child is in the position of witnessing sexual sin and then informs the betrayed parent or confronts the offending parent, it is more likely they will feel responsible for the ensuing disruption in the family because they had an active role in the sin coming to light. They will need consistent reassurance that they did not cause the disruption. Ideally, this reassurance should come from both parents as well as the adult individual identified as supporter of the children.

Notes

STEP 1, PART ONE
1. Carlo DiClemente, *Addiction and Change* (Guilford Press, 2003).

STEP 1, PART TWO
1. More information about The Sexual and Gender Identity Institute can be found at https://www.wheaton.edu/academics/school-of-psychology-counseling-and-family-therapy/sexual-and-gender-identity-institute/.

STEP 1, PART THREE
1. Ed Welch, *Crossroads: A Step-by-Step Guide Away from Addiction* (New Growth Press, 2008), 33, 36.

2. Earl Wilson, Sandy Wilson, Paul Friesen, Virginia Friesen, Larry Paulson, and Nancy Paulson, *Restoring the Fallen: A Team Approach to Caring, Confronting & Reconciling* (InterVarsity Press, 1997), 29.

3. Tim Chester, *Closing the Window: Steps to Living Porn Free* (InterVarsity Press, 2010), 24.

4. Steve Gallagher, *At the Altar of Sexual Idolatry* (Pure Life Ministries, 2016), 50.

5. Chester, *Closing the Window*, 120–25.

6. Doug Rosenau, *A Celebration of Sex* (Thomas Nelson, 2002), 348.

7. If you are not aware of a local G4 group, information for finding a counselor or support group to help you in your journey can be found at bradhambrick.com/findacounselor.

STEP 2, PART ONE
1. Tim Challies, *Sexual Detox: A Guide for Guys Who Are Sick of Porn* (Cruciform Press, 2010), 17.

2. David Powlison, *Pornography: Slaying the Dragon* (P&R Publishing, 1999), 16.

3. Robert D. Jones, *Restoring Your Broken Marriage: Healing After Adultery* (P&R Publishing, 2009), 8–9.

4. Doug Rosenau, *A Celebration of Sex* (Thomas Nelson, 2002), 349.

5. Mark Laaser, *Healing the Wounds of Sexual Addiction* (Zondervan, 2004), 62, 153.

6. Gary Shriver and Mona Shriver, *Unfaithful: Hope and Healing After Infidelity,* (David C. Cook, 2009), 148.

STEP 2, PART TWO
1. Naomi Wolf, "The Porn Myth," *New York Magazine*, October 9, 2003. Online at https://nymag.com/nymetro/news/trends/n_9437/.

2. Harry Schaumburg, *False Intimacy* (NavPress, 1997), 40.

3. Schaumburg, *False Intimacy*, 46.

4. Mark Laaser, *Healing the Wounds of Sexual Addiction* (Zondervan, 2004), 66.

5. Tim Chester, *Closing the Window: Steps to Living Porn Free* (InterVarsity Press, 2010), 91–92.

6. Cornelius Plantinga Jr., *Not the Way It's Supposed to Be: A Breviary of Sin* (William B. Eerdmans, 1996), 131.

STEP 2, PART THREE

1. Stefanie Carnes, ed., *Mending a Shattered Heart* (Gentle Path Press, 2011), 27.

STEP 3, PART TWO

1. Tim Challies, *Sexual Detox: A Guide for Guys Who Are Sick of Porn* (Cruciform Press, 2010), 61.

STEP 4, PART ONE

1. A. W. Tozer, *The Knowledge of the Holy* (HarperCollins, 2018), 1.

2. C. S. Lewis, *Mere Christianity* (HarperCollins, 2001), 53–54.

3. John Piper, *Future Grace* (Multnomah, 1995), 336.

4. Brad Hambrick, *Making Sense of Forgiveness: Moving from Hurt Toward Hope* (New Growth Press, 2021). For guidance and grappling with guilt and self-forgiveness, see chapters 6–8 and 16–17.

5. David Powlison, *Sexual Addiction: Freedom from Compulsive Behavior* (New Growth Press, 2010), 15–16.

6. Summary adapted from C. S. Lewis, *The Great Divorce* (HarperCollins, 2001), 106–15.

7. Tim Chester, *Closing the Window: Steps to Living Porn Free* (InterVarsity Press, 2010), 70.

STEP 4, PART TWO

1. Mark Laaser, *Healing the Wounds of Sexual Addiction* (Zondervan, 2004), 24.

2. Tim Chester, *Closing the Window: Steps to Living Porn Free* (InterVarsity Press, 2010), 57, 68.

3. David Powlison, *Pornography: Slaying the Dragon* (P&R Publishing, 1999), 20.

4. Laaser, *Healing the Wounds of Sexual Addiction*, 24.

STEP 5, PART ONE

1. David White, "Living in the Light: A Redemptive Response to Sexual Sin," Harvest USA, January 15, 2014, https://harvestusa.org/living-in-the-light-a-redemptive-response-to-sexual-sin/.

2. Brad Hambrick, *Transformative Friendships: 7 Questions to Deepen Any Relationship* (New Growth Press, 2024).

STEP 5, PART TWO

1. These points adapted from Ken Sande, *Peacemaking for Families* (Focus on the Family, 2002). I highly recommend this book as you seek to restore health in your relationships with family and friends.

STEP 6, PART ONE

1. David Powlison, *Sexual Addiction: Freedom from Compulsive Behavior* (New Growth Press, 2010), 25.

STEP 6, PART TWO

1. Mark Laaser, *Healing the Wounds of Sexual Addiction* (Zondervan, 2004), 165.

STEP 6, PART THREE

1. Brad Hambrick, *Angry with God: An Honest Journey Through Suffering and Betrayal* (New Growth Press, 2022). See especially chapter 11 for a discussion on the theme of primary and secondary emotions.

2. David Powlison, *Pornography: Slaying the Dragon* (P&R Publishing, 1999), 13.

3. Doug Rosenau, *A Celebration of Sex* (Thomas Nelson, 2002), 355.

4. Tim Chester, *Closing the Window: Steps to Living Porn Free* (InterVarsity Press, 2010), 18.

5. Mark Laaser, *Healing the Wounds of Sexual Addiction* (Zondervan, 2004), 26.

STEP 6, PART FOUR

1. Kent Dunnington, *Addiction and Virtue: Beyond the Models of Disease and Choice* (IVP Academic, 2011), 178.

STEP 7, PART ONE

1. These four phases of relapse are adapted from Stephen Arterburn and Linda Mintle, *Lose It for Life* (Thomas Nelson, 2011), 228–30. The categories given in the original book are complacency, confusion, compromise, and catastrophe.

STEP 7, PART TWO

1. David Powlison, *Sexual Addiction: Freedom from Compulsive Behavior* (New Growth, 2010), 8–10.

STEP 7, PART THREE

1. The series Creating a Gospel-Centered Marriage is designed for both marital enrichment and marital preparation. As an extension of *False Love*, the material can be utilized for marital enrichment after this season of marital restoration work.

2. Joel Belz, quoted in Rusty Benson, "Half A Poison Pill Won't Kill Me: Thoughts on Worldliness and the Media that Promote It," *AFA Journal,* May 2002, https://afajournal.org/past-issues/2002/may/half-a-poison-pill-won-t-kill-me/.

STEP 8, PART ONE

1. C. S. Lewis, *Mere Christianity* (HarperCollins, 2001), 142.

STEP 8, PART THREE

1. Brad Hambrick, *Transformative Friendships: 7 Questions to Deepen Any Relationship* (New Growth Press, 2024).

2. Michael Emlet, *Saints, Sufferers, and Sinners: Loving Others as God Loves Us* (New Growth Press, 2021).